Evaluating Faculty Performance

Evaluating Faculty Performance

A Practical Guide to Assessing Teaching, Research, and Service

Peter Seldin
Pace University

and Associates

ANKER PUBLISHING COMPANY, INC.
Bolton, Massachusetts

Evaluating Faculty Performance
A Practical Guide to Assessing Teaching, Research, and Service

ISBN 1-933371-04-8

Composition by Jessica Holland
Cover design by Dutton and Sherman Design

Anker Publishing Company, Inc.
563 Main Street
P.O. Box 249
Bolton, MA 01740-0249 USA

www.ankerpub.com

Library of Congress Cataloging-in-Publication Data

Seldin, Peter.
  Evaluating faculty performance : a practical guide to assessing teaching, research, and service / Peter Seldin.
      p. cm.
  Includes bibliographical references and index.
  ISBN 1-933371-04-8
  1. College teachers—Rating of. 2. College teaching—Evaluation. I. Title.

LB2333.S438 2006
378.1'24—dc22
                              2006000981

Table of Contents

About the Author

Peter Seldin is Distinguished Professor of Management Emeritus at Pace University in Pleasantville, New York. A behavioral scientist, educator, author, and specialist in evaluation and development of faculty and administrative performance, he has been a consultant on higher education issues to more than 350 colleges and universities throughout the United States and in 45 countries around the world.

A well-known speaker at national and international conferences, Dr. Seldin regularly serves as a faculty leader in programs offered by the American Council on Education and AACSB International (Association to Advance Collegiate Schools of Business) and is codirector of the annual International Conference on Improving University Teaching.

His well-received books include:

The Teaching Portfolio, third edition (Anker, 2004)

The Administrative Portfolio, with Mary Lou Higgerson (Anker, 2002)

Changing Practices in Evaluating Teaching, with associates (Anker, 1999)

The Teaching Portfolio, second edition (Anker, 1997)

Improving College Teaching, with associates (Anker, 1995)

Successful Use of Teaching Portfolios, with associates (Anker, 1993)

The Teaching Portfolio (Anker, 1991)

How Administrators Can Improve Teaching, with associates (Jossey-Bass, 1990)

Evaluating and Developing Administrative Performance (Jossey-Bass, 1988)

Coping with Faculty Stress, with associates (Jossey-Bass, 1987)

Changing Practices in Faculty Evaluation (Jossey-Bass, 1984)

Successful Faculty Evaluation Programs (Coventry Press, 1980)

Teaching Professors to Teach (Blythe-Pennington, 1977)
How Colleges Evaluate Professors (Blythe-Pennington, 1975)

He has contributed numerous articles on the teaching profession, student ratings, educational practice, and academic culture to such publications as *The New York Times, The Chronicle of Higher Education,* and *Change* magazine. Among recent honors, he was named by the World Bank as a visiting scholar to Indonesia. In addition, he was elected a fellow of the College of Preceptors in London, England. This special honor is given to a small number of faculty and administrators who are judged to have made an "outstanding contribution to higher education on the international level." For his contributions to the scholarship of teaching, he has received honorary degrees from Keystone College (Pennsylvania) and Columbia College (South Carolina).

About the Contributors

Monica A. Devanas has been teaching microbiology courses at Rutgers University since 1984. She began teaching Biomedical Issues of HIV/AIDS in 1992, and in 2001 the course was recognized as a national model for Science Education for New Civic Engagements and Responsibilities (SENCER.net). She is director of faculty development and assessment programs at the Center for Advancement of Teaching, where she assists faculty in all aspects of pedagogy, in particular teaching portfolios.

George B. Ellenberg is associate dean of the College of Arts and Sciences at the University of West Florida. He has been active in university accreditation and enhancing the university's general studies program. In addition to his administrative duties, he teaches courses in military history and in his specialty, the American south. He has taught and observed secondary-level student teachers in history and social studies for several years, and has been the recipient of numerous teaching awards from the middle school to university level.

David Fite is associate provost for institutional planning and assessment at Chapman University. Previously, he served as professor of English and director of the Faculty Center for Professional Development at California State Polytechnic University–Pomona. He is author of *Harold Bloom: The Rhetoric of Romantic Vision* (University of Massachusetts Press, 1985) and numerous articles on rhetoric, literary theory, and modern poetics. He has served as a consultant on faculty development, learning outcomes assessment, program review, and institutional accreditation for many colleges and universities.

Jane S. Halonen is dean of the College of Arts and Sciences and professor of psychology at the University of West Florida. She has taught and served as an administrator at Alverno College and James Madison University and was a consultant to the American Psychological Association on various projects dealing with student learning outcomes. Her scholarly expertise is reflected in publications on assessment, critical thinking, and faculty development as well as in psychology and student success textbooks.

Mary Lou Higgerson is vice president for academic affairs and dean of the college at Baldwin-Wallace College. Before 2000, she served for 27 years on the faculty and in a variety of administrative positions at Southern Illinois University–Carbondale, where she was named distinguished teacher in 1997. She has authored numerous books and articles for practicing administrators and has presented on leadership communication topics at the American Council on Education's National Leadership Seminars for chairs and deans and for other organizations and institutions.

Teck-Kah Lim is professor of physics and associate vice provost for graduate studies at Drexel University. An American Physical Society Fellow, he served for four years as the secretary/treasurer of its Topical Group on Few-Body Systems and Multiparticle Dynamics. In that capacity he helped to decide on the group's fellowship nominees. For two years he was the Drexel University counselor and he chaired the university's appeals committee on tenure during that period. He has served on numerous tenure and promotion committees over the years.

Thomas V. McGovern cofounded the Department of Integrative Studies at Arizona State University (ASU) in 1990. As president of the Arizona Faculty Council, he helped negotiate a post-tenure review system with the board of regents in 1997–1998. He is a fellow of the American Psychological Association and the American Psychological Society. He was CASE/Carnegie Foundation Professor of the Year in Arizona (2003), received the Faculty Award for Achievement in Service at ASU West (1997), and the Distinguished Teaching Award at Virginia Commonwealth University (1988).

J. Elizabeth Miller is associate professor of child and family studies at Northern Illinois University. Previously, she was the university director of the Office of Teaching Assistant Training and Development, where she established and ran the training program for more than 800 teaching assistants. She is the recipient of several teaching and service awards and is the outgoing chair of the Women's Caucus of the former American Association for Higher Education. Her research focuses on the interplay between feminist teaching and learner-centered teaching.

Barbara J. Millis has been active in faculty development since 1982 and currently serves as the director of the Excellence in Teaching Program at the University of Nevada–Reno. She has published extensively in many areas of faculty development such as cooperative learning, classroom observations, microteaching, classroom assessment/research, and academic assessment. She is coauthor (with Phillip Cottell) of *Cooperative Learning for Higher Education Faculty* (ACE/Oryx Press, 1998) and (with John Hertel) *Using Simulations to Enhance Learning in Higher Education* (Stylus, 2002).

William Pallett has served as director of The IDEA Center (Individual Development and Educational Assessment Center) since 1997. Prior to that, he served as director of assessment and codirector of the Office of Educational Advancement at Kansas State University. Since joining the center, he has been involved in all phases of the student rating system's development and research. He regularly provides telephone consultation to clients and has conducted IDEA training workshops at more than 50 colleges and universities.

Clement A. Seldin is professor of education at the University of Massachusetts Amherst, where he teaches courses in the foundations of American education. His research has focused on parent/teacher communication and selectivity in teacher education. In addition, he has worked with Columbia University Teachers College on two major studies of schools of education. He is the recipient of several teaching honors including the University Distinguished Teaching Award and the College Outstanding Teaching Award.

Todd Zakrajsek is the inaugural director of the Faculty Center for Innovative Teaching at Central Michigan University. Previously, he was the founding director of the Center for Teaching and Learning at Southern Oregon University, where he also taught in the psychology department as a tenured associate professor. He has published and presented widely on the topic of student learning.

John Zubizarreta is professor of English and director of honors and faculty development at Columbia College (South Carolina). He has earned several teaching and scholarly awards, including recognition as a CASE/Carnegie Foundation Professor of the Year in South Carolina (1994), and he publishes widely on American and comparative literatures, teaching and learning, academic leadership, honors education, and portfolio development.

Preface

An important change is taking place in higher education. Faculty members are being held accountable, as never before, for how well they do their jobs. Current interest in appraising faculty performance in teaching, research, and service grows out of the demand by the government, general public, and every sector of the academic community for more accountability. It also stems from the growth of faculty power—unionization on the one hand, and shared governance on the other—which increases the demand for a visible and equitable (by faculty measures) evaluation system.

Why should a college or university undertake the difficult, time-consuming, and costly process of systematically evaluating faculty performance? One compelling reason is that evaluation of performance, when done well, helps identify areas that need fine-tuning. As a result, the institution, the faculty member, and his or her students all benefit.

Another important reason for institutions to develop more rational and fair approaches to the evaluation of faculty performance is to provide a firm basis for tenure, promotion, and retention decisions. With annual salaries plus benefits for senior faculty typically ranging from $50,000 to $150,000, such decisions can have significant financial implications.

Evaluating Faculty Performance offers faculty members and administrators the practical, ready-to-use, research-based information required to foster truly effective and equitable evaluation at their institutions. This book is a reasoned, well-grounded guide for achieving needed changes in evaluation and development of faculty performance in teaching, research, and service.

Earlier books on faculty evaluation have taken a broad, how-to approach and have been geared primarily to institutions that are just setting up their faculty evaluation programs. The focus here is different. This book:

- Describes the key elements of existing systems that must be improved in order to strengthen the overall system
- Addresses how to establish the right climate for evaluation
- Identifies best practices in evaluating teaching, research, and service
- Discusses the professional portfolio as a way of documenting faculty performance
- Reveals what *not* to do in evaluating performance
- Outlines key issues, red-flag dangers, and benchmarks for success

In short, *Evaluating Faculty Performance* offers college and university faculty and administrators the kind of pragmatic, hands-on information about specific strategies and state-of-the-art techniques required to improve faculty performance. This book presents promising new approaches for assessing and improving faculty potential, practical recommendations for action, and 12 field-tested forms designed to sharpen the evaluation of faculty performance. The aim is to generate objective and critical thinking and, where necessary, to act as a stimulus for change.

This book is written for presidents, academic vice presidents, provosts, deans, department chairs, instructional development specialists, and faculty—the essential partners in evaluating faculty performance. The practical suggestions and recommendations should prove of value to these faculty and administrators whether they are in public or private institutions. The language used is straightforward and nontechnical. This book distills not only the literature but also the broad-based personal experience of each contributor. In addition to being experts in their fields, almost all contributors have held teaching and administrative positions and, consequently, have been on both sides of faculty evaluation.

Overview of the Contents

Chapter 1. Peter Seldin discusses the major requirements needed to construct a faculty evaluation program, as well as the reasons for evaluating performance and the barriers to doing so. He examines the evaluation of teaching, research, and service and identifies the common characteristics found in successful evaluation programs.

Chapter 2. Peter Seldin explains that effective evaluation programs should follow key operating principles and provides guidelines for the psychological and general process of evaluation. He cites deficiencies commonly found in evaluation programs, lists necessary precautions that must be taken, and presents a detailed, composite summary of institutions that have improved their evaluation programs.

Chapter 3. Mary Lou Higgerson argues that engaging faculty in per-formance *counseling* instead of performance *evaluation* is essential for building a climate that improves performance. She discusses the importance of setting concrete and specific performance expecta-tions, describes how to establish expectations for continuous review, and uses case studies to illuminate key points.

Chapter 4. William Pallett examines the uses and abuses of student ratings. He contends that they are a valuable resource but should count just 30% to 50% in the overall evaluation of teaching, that such ratings can serve multiple purposes, that administrators some-times make too much of too little difference in ratings, and that stu-dent rating results should be categorized into no more than three to five groups.

Chapter 5. Clement A. Seldin argues that faculty should determine how institutional service is valued by the department or institution. He suggests that faculty should participate in internal and external service, document their service contributions by providing detailed evidence of their active engagement, and identify and describe leadership positions.

Chapter 6. Barbara J. Millis argues that collegial peer classroom observations are an effective strategy to improve teaching, describes the four-step process for doing so, and discusses the benefits of developing a common department observation instrument. She outlines three useful models for involving departments in the design of a common observation instrument.

Chapter 7. Thomas V. McGovern explores how an academic life narrative can lead to self-determined renewal and continuing self-evaluation for faculty. He discusses the importance of continuously recalibrating the balance among teaching, research, and service commitments across the academic life span and offers dozens of reflective prompt questions for goal-setting, faculty discussion, and the composition of an academic life narrative.

Chapter 8. Monica A. Devanas explains why the teaching portfolio is an especially good vehicle for evaluating teaching. She offers concrete examples of the evidence that might be included, differentiates between portfolios for improvement and portfolios for personnel decisions, and argues that a mentor is the best asset a faculty member can have when completing a teaching portfolio.

Chapter 9. Teck-Kah Lim presents the essential elements in evaluating faculty research, explains why evaluators must have a reasonable idea of how research is practiced in different disciplines, and discusses the scholarship of teaching and learning. He examines quantitative performance indicators and argues that composite measures, bibliometric indicators, and peer review all have a place in the evaluation of research.

Chapter 10. Jane S. Halonen and George B. Ellenberg argue that folly too often characterizes evaluative practices by students, faculty, and administrators. They provide specific examples of how students can be unduly harsh in their feedback and describe specific strategies that administrators can use to contextualize such comments so faculty can extract ideas for improvement with minimal pain.

Chapter 11. Todd Zakrajsek identifies best practices in using evaluation data to improve performance. He explains why advice for seasoned faculty is often very different from advice for new faculty, discusses how faculty colleagues can help improve performance, and provides suggestions for faculty who are trying to better their teaching.

Chapter 12. David Fite outlines best practices in using evaluation data for tenure, promotion, and retention decisions. He addresses the critical importance of established and widely understood performance standards and criteria, stresses reliance on multiple evaluation sources and types of evidence, discusses due process, and identifies the vital link between evaluation and faculty mentoring and development.

Chapter 13. John Zubizarreta describes the professional portfolio, an evidence-based document in which the faculty member reflects on, concisely organizes, and records selective details of teaching, research, and service, the often competing dimensions of faculty responsibility. He discusses evidence that might be included, differentiates it from traditional end-of-the-year activity reports, and argues that the value of the professional portfolio can be extended to students, support staff, and administration.

Chapter 14. J. Elizabeth Miller summarizes the key points and recommendations of each chapter. These suggestions can help faculty and administrators bring about much-needed improvement in the evaluation of faculty performance. Collectively, the recommendations represent best practices in the evaluation of faculty teaching, research, and service.

Appendix. Compiled by J. Elizabeth Miller, this section contains tested and proven evaluation forms.

Peter Seldin
Pleasantville, New York
February 2006

Building a Successful Evaluation Program

1

Peter Seldin

Evaluating faculty performance is hardly new on campus. It has always had a place in academic history, if only by inference or casual observation. Students have sized up their professor's strengths and weaknesses and passed their appraisals on to other students. Faculty members have picked up impressions of a colleague's competence from bits and pieces of evidence and exchanged their views with their peers. And administrators have pulled together informal impressions of the skills and personal attributes of individual faculty members and shared their impressions with their fellow administrators.

What is new at colleges and universities, however, is the attempt to root out casual bias, hearsay evidence, and gossip—the hallmarks of traditional organizations—in favor of a more systematic and objective approach to evaluating faculty performance. Continuing tight budgets have forced institutions to rethink the ways they evaluate faculty performance in an effort to separate high-performing faculty from their mediocre or low-performing colleagues. Such efforts are admirable.

Faculty evaluation has many facets. It is an exercise in observation and judgment. It is a measurement and feedback process. It is an inexact, human method that must meet key requirements if it is to succeed.

Key Requirements

When constructing a program to evaluate faculty performance, some key requirements should be observed.

Practicality
Evaluation instruments should be readily understood and easily used by administrators, faculty, students, and others involved in the process. They should not demand an inordinate amount of time or energy, and they should not have to be completed too often.

Relevance
There should be clear links between institutional goals and the criteria and standards for faculty performance. For example, an institution that has a goal of being a teaching institution should not expect faculty members to produce a scholarly book every year or two. Relevance can be determined by answering the question—What *really* makes the difference between success and failure in a faculty position at this institution?

Comprehensive Evaluation
All relevant components of a faculty member's performance should be identified and included in the evaluation program. For most faculty today, the relevant areas include teaching, research/publication, and service. Even components that are time-consuming or tend to defy measurement should not be overlooked.

Sensitivity
The issue here is whether the evaluation system is capable of really distinguishing effective from ineffective performance. If not, effective faculty will be rated on par with mediocre ones, and the evaluation system will be not be helpful for improving performance or personnel decisions. There is an important difference between an evaluation program designed for development purposes and one designed for personnel decisions. The system designed to promote improved performance requires data about differences *within* individual faculty members whereas the system designed for personnel decisions (such as tenure, promotion, and retention) requires data

about differences *between* individuals. The two patterns of information are like two keys that open different doors.

Freedom From Contamination

The performance of a faculty member should be measured without the contamination of factors clearly beyond his or her control, such as faulty or inadequate equipment. The purpose is to evaluate the faculty member's performance without holding him or her responsible for extraneous factors.

Reliability

Consistency of judgment is needed if the evaluations are to be trusted. It stands to reason that raters from different vantage points (e.g., students, faculty colleagues, department chairs) will perceive the performance of a given faculty member differently. Their appraisals may not coincide exactly, but they should be in general agreement. Each offers a unique perspective, and together, one hopes, they paint a complete picture of the faculty member's performance.

Acceptability

This is perhaps the most important requirement of all. It is the foundation upon which the evaluation system rests. Unless the evaluation program has the full support of both the evaluators and those being evaluated, it will likely fail. Too many colleges and universities focus their attention on the technical soundness of the program rather than on its attitudinal and interpersonal aspects. Success for the evaluation program will be much more likely if institutions court campus personnel, engage them in frank discussions, and make a serious effort to garner active support for the program on campus.

Why Evaluate Faculty Performance?

The cornerstone of every faculty evaluation program is its purpose. The purpose influences the sources of data, the kind of information gathered, the depth of data analysis, and the dissemination of findings. In colleges and universities today there are two primary reasons to evaluate faculty members: 1) to improve their performance, and 2) to provide a rational and equitable basis for personnel decisions.

Evaluation to Improve Performance

There is no better reason to evaluate than to improve performance. Evaluation provides data to assist the faltering, to motivate the tired, and to encourage the indecisive. Faculty members are hired by institutions in expectation of first-class performance. To help them hone their performance is simply a logical extension of this expectation. Just as students need feedback and guidance to correct errors, so faculty need factual data and helpful direction if they are to improve their performance.

Whether such improvement actually takes place, however, depends largely on the facts turned up by the evaluation. It will not work unless the elements to be improved are specifically singled out. And even then, the faculty member must genuinely care about the evaluation process and realistically be able to make the changes. Simply handing a professor the results of, say, student evaluations is unlikely to bring about significant changes. A follow-up injection of short periods of faculty counseling may be needed.

To help accomplish this, many colleges and universities have created faculty development centers, staffed by instructional consultants, to bring advice and guidance to faculty members interested in converting evaluative feedback into teaching improvement. A professor asking for help will work one-on-one with a consultant. Feedback on his or her teaching performance will come from many sources: a sample of instructional material, classroom observation, a videotaped classroom session, student evaluation, instructor self-assessment. After a joint analysis by the consultant and the faculty member, the teaching skill or skills needing improvement will be identified and corrective action planned. A basic test of the willingness of a college or university to help faculty members improve performance is its willingness to provide such support.

Performance evaluation need not be restricted to the classroom. It is equally applicable to the professor's role as a scholar engaged in research and publication, or as a member of the college or university community engaged in community or institutional service. The process is the same. It includes gathering detailed data from a range of sources, joint analysis of the data by the professor and an esteemed colleague or consultant, and planning and implementing the corrective action. The confidentiality of the data gathered must remain inviolate. If such data is shared, it must be with the consultant and at the discretion of the appraised professor. For data gathered for improvement purposes to be surreptitiously used for personnel decisions would have an immediately chilling, even fatal, effect on the credibility of the entire evaluation program.

In an ideal world, faculty evaluation would be conducted separately for the purpose of improving teaching and making personnel decisions, since one may have great impact on the other. But because of vital time and financial constraints, many institutions conduct them simultaneously by integrating into a single questionnaire both the core items useful to administrators in personnel decisions and selected items useful to the faculty member to improve performance. Who receives which feedback? Professors are given their rating results on all items, but administrators are given results only of the core items.

Evaluation for Personnel Decisions

Another reason for evaluating faculty performance is to provide a rational, equitable basis for crucial administrative decisions on tenure, promotion in rank, and retention. These decisions have always been made by colleges and universities, but in recent years many institutions have moved faculty evaluation for personnel decisions to the top of their list of reasons for assessing performance. With salaries plus benefits for senior faculty typically ranging from $50,000 to $150,000, personnel decisions to promote or tenure can have significant financial implications.

In their pursuit of sound administrative decisions, many institutions have stumbled in setting up evaluation programs. In haste, some inaccurate data-gathering methods and instruments have been adopted with the inevitable result of flawed decisions. Practices on many campuses are marred by a get-it-done-quickly approach to faculty evaluation. As a senior faculty member at an eastern university commented recently, "The provost wanted feedback on the performance of a new faculty member and he wanted it in any form we wanted to give it, within five days."

Faculty members are in general agreement that deadwood needs elimination from their ranks. But they balk at what they consider a nonobjective screening process, especially one done in haste.

Without doubt, the two primary reasons for faculty evaluation are to improve performance and to assist in personnel decisions. But there is an additional reason for assessing faculty performance worth mentioning: providing data to interested individuals and organizations operating off campus.

Evaluation to Provide Data to Outsiders

Boards of trustees, parents, taxpayers, and government officials have demanded all sorts of data on institutional and faculty efficiency. In many states, legislation requires colleges and universities to prepare and maintain detailed records on faculty hiring, promotion, retention, and tenure. For this reason, it makes sense for institutions to collect and disseminate information on students served, student learning and satisfaction ratings, drop-out and matriculation rates, alumni employment and achievement patterns, and community and social contributions.

Barriers to Evaluating Faculty Performance

To say that the evaluation of faculty performance is useful is one thing. To get it off the ground and keep it running smoothly is another. First, there are social and attitudinal problems. Some academics persist in the argument that they are unique and therefore not subject to evaluation. They argue that direct observation of their teaching is an invasion of professional privacy and that peer reviewers of their research/scholarship are not able to know their intent. But evaluation of performance is an inherent element of any organized effort to achieve a goal. If we do not submit to and cooperate with rational types of evaluation, we will be evaluated by hearsay evidence, gossip, and other shoddy means.

Second, there is the immediate problem of developing accurate measuring rods of faculty performance. This is no simple matter. It is disheartening to see how the use of unreliable methods, vague criteria, and uncertain performance standards have undermined faith and confidence in faculty evaluation. Just because the measurement of performance is inherently difficult is not reason to consider the problem insurmountable. Such reasoning makes it easy to rationalize away the need for faculty appraisal (Seldin, 2005).

Third, other opponents of evaluation argue that teaching is too complex and subjective to be evaluated. McKeachie and Seldin (2005) dispose of this argument by saying that it is the very complexity of teaching that makes every bit of empirical evidence the more precious.

Fourth, there is the unspoken professorial dislike of being judged. This is natural. Professors, like most human beings, tend to regard an appraisal as an implicit threat. Since evaluation can be ill-defined and threatening and sometimes result in unfair judgments, their resistance needs some sympathetic understanding. A trade-off approach that emphasizes the positive values to faculty members in enhancing their performance seems to work best. Further, it's better to be judged systematically and with reasonable justice than by the haphazard methods of the past (Seldin, 2004).

Fifth, some additional obstacles to effective evaluation are destructive enough to warrant special mention.

- Standards and ratings are mercurial and tend to fluctuate wide-ly—and sometimes unfairly. Some raters are tough. Others are lenient. Thus the less competent in one academic department can be awarded a higher rating than the more competent in another department.

- Instead of bestowing negative ratings or below-average salary increases on less effective faculty members, some evaluators take the easy way out by assigning an average or even above-average rating on inferior performance.

- Excessive emphasis is sometimes placed on numbers. Some eval-uators have a numbers fetish. They venerate numbers and use them as though they were hard, objective facts.

This is a daunting list of barriers and obstacles, one which can give pause to any college or university contemplating the introduc-tion or upgrading of an existing faculty evaluation program. Yet it is no solution to decide *not* to introduce or upgrade the program. Why? Because off-the-cuff evaluations will always be made. Even with the barriers and obstacles, it is better to install a program that requires evaluations to approach fairness and accuracy.

No one will argue that absolute precision and objectivity in fac-ulty evaluation is foreseeable. But to eliminate faculty appraisal because today's techniques of getting at it are less than perfect is not an answer. Light from a single candle is more helpful in finding our way than total darkness. Two candles are better. The object is to add candles and steadily and collectively increase the illumination.

Evaluating Teaching

Some professors still argue that teaching cannot be evaluated because no one knows even how to define effective teaching. They automatically downgrade the growing number of scholarly investigations that are sorting out effective and ineffective teaching behaviors. The hallmarks of good teaching are reasonably consistent in most studies. They include being well-prepared for class, demonstrating comprehensive subject knowledge, motivating students, being fair and reasonable in managing the details of learning, and being sincerely interested in the subject matter and in teaching itself. How can the presence or absence of these qualities in a professor be known? Students, faculty colleagues, administrators, and faculty members themselves each play a key role in the collective evaluation of teaching performance.

Students can provide reliable and valid appraisals of both the course and the instructor, provided the questions they are asked are appropriate and properly answerable by students and the rating forms are properly prepared and administered (see Chapters 4, 10, 11, and 13).

Faculty colleagues can offer insights into an instructor's performance through classroom observation or by reviewing the professor's teaching materials, such as the syllabi, handouts, tests, homework assignments, reading lists, term papers, and lab reports (see Chapter 6).

Administrators—department chairs and deans—are an important source of teaching evaluation, even though they rarely venture into the classroom and therefore rely on their own informational sources for judgments on effective teaching (see Chapter 3).

Faculty self-evaluation, if carefully and honestly performed, contributes to the accuracy and reliability of the collective judgment of teaching effectiveness, and is an immediate and effective impetus to improve teaching performance (see Chapter 9).

Evaluating Research and Publication

Most institutions expect their faculty members to be dedicated to the classroom and solidly involved in research and publication. Faculty are accountable in both areas. Unfortunately, at many colleges and universities, research and publication is not evaluated; it is merely counted. What enters the numerical count, however, differs from institution to institution. Some count only the so-called refereed journals and thus relegate to the academic dustbin some excellent nonrefereed publications. Others count only research-based articles and dismiss theoretical articles no matter how noteworthy (see Chapter 9).

Complicating the matter still further, at many colleges and universities research and publication is put through different kinds of evaluative wringers. There is committee evaluation, national reputation of the author, journal quality, reference citation in other publications, and on-campus reputation. Confusion reigns in institutions that have not established categories of articles and publications. The result is that considerable uncertainty exists in the minds of the professors and the committee members evaluating them as to just what is and is not important. The problem is often more acute in colleges and universities where members sit on institution-wide tenure and promotion committees and are asked to evaluate the research performance of faculty members who are not from their academic discipline (Seldin, 2005).

Evaluating Institutional Service and Student Advising

Faculty members are expected to serve on institutional committees such as those concerned with policy, recruitment, tenure and promotion, and student affairs. It is taken as an article of faith that all faculty members on all committees are operating at peak efficiency. So when decisions on tenure, promotion, and retention are being made, the length of a professor's committee list is automatically translated into the size of his or her contribution to the institution. The longer the list, the greater the contribution. In this alchemy, quantity is translated into quality (see Chapter 5).

Although most institutions include student advising as institutional service, it receives only passing attention from most tenure and promotion committees. However, a small number of colleges and universities have developed the criteria and standards needed to appraise the quality of a professor's contribution as student advisor, including advisor knowledge, availability, interest in students, referral to other sources when appropriate, clear presentation of information, helping to resolve students' nonacademic problems, and student satisfaction.

Implementing Faculty Evaluation Programs

How an evaluation program is put into place is just as critical as *what* program is used. Consider the brash approach used by the provost of a midwestern university. Convinced that a revised faculty evaluation program was needed, the provost sent a set of detailed forms and the following memo to all faculty: "It is the policy of this university to evaluate the performance of all faculty members each year. Effective immediately, all faculty will use the enclosed forms for that purpose. I look forward to the success of the program." The groundswell of protest was strong and immediate, and the surprised provost withdrew the memo within a few months. Too often, faculty evaluation programs are introduced by administrative fiat, even though this virtually dooms the program to failure.

A series of carefully planned steps are needed to implement a performance evaluation program. Just as two individuals do not cross a brook in the same way, no two institutions will implement an improved evaluation program in the same way. However, there are certain steps that are crucial to success in the implantation of all evaluation programs.

Examine the Givens

According to Seldin (2005), the following questions must be considered before initiating a redesign effort to improve an existing faculty evaluation program:

- Why are we really thinking about redesigning the program?
- What organizational commitment is behind the redesign effort?
- What can we realistically expect to accomplish within a specified timeframe?
- Do we have sufficient resources, financial and human, to carry out the effort?
- How and why is it important to redesign the evaluation system now in place?

Select a Development Group

Those selected as members of the development group must be knowledgeable and favorably oriented to the task. But they must also have credibility with the faculty and the administration. The group should be kept small, about five to eight individuals, and should include both senior and junior participants as well as human resource department specialists.

Review Institutional Evaluation Practices

Prior to redesigning the evaluation program, the development group should review the institution's current appraisal policies and practices. The group should also look into other feedback systems, legal issues, institutional philosophy, and organizational climate. Questionnaires are sometimes used to determine opinion on what is working and what is not and to elicit recommendations for improvement.

Evaluate the Organizational Context

Evaluation systems do not operate in a vacuum—they interact with every part of the college or university. That's why it is so important that the evaluation program be:

- Consistent with the institution's philosophy and practice
- Consistent with the nature of faculty work patterns
- In compliance with legal issues
- Administered at a high level in the institution
- Positively linked with institutional rewards for compensation, tenure, and promotion
- Given active and public support by top-level administrators and faculty leaders

Develop a Redesigned Program

Only after examining givens and evaluating contextual factors should the development group turn its attention to the process of redesigning a program. This process typically involves drafting performance evaluation policy, developing appropriate forms, establishing suitable procedures, and testing the measurement/feedback/developmental needs/monitoring loop to see if it fits together.

Use Open Communication

No faculty evaluation system stands much chance of success unless it is candidly and fully explained to faculty and administration and, most important, successful in winning their acceptance. Sugarcoating or obfuscating explanation dooms the program to failure. Every step of the program must be openly arrived at, fully explained, and widely publicized. Every doubt must be resolved; every question answered satisfactorily. Open faculty forums are especially helpful for analyzing and discussing draft documents and for distributing progress reports as the evaluation system develops. Using open communication means that every faculty member knows accurately and completely the criteria, standards, and evidence needed for salary increase, promotion, and tenure. It also means complete knowledge of institutional policies and procedures in performance evaluation.

A Guide to Successful Faculty Evaluation

Colleges and universities would enjoy nothing better than faculty excellence. What prevents it? Why isn't it achieved? First, because evaluative criteria are general and therefore hard to pin down, at too many institutions professors operate in the semi-dark about how their performance will be evaluated. The inevitable result: an unfortunate mixture of faculty disillusion and confusion. Second, faculty members face frustration as they try to juggle teaching, research, publication, public service, student advising, and campus committees to the satisfaction of their institutions and academic departments. They also have their own personal interests to pursue and their own private lives.

What steps must a college or university take to develop a faculty evaluation program that is flexible, comprehensive, and fair? What common characteristics routinely appear in successful evaluation programs? The following guidelines may act as therapy for ailing evaluation programs.

Deciding the System's Purpose

It is crucial to decide at the outset which purpose the evaluation program is to serve. One purpose is to improve faculty performance. Another is to provide useful data on which to base personnel decisions. A third is to yield requested data to interested individuals, government agencies, and accrediting bodies. Because these purposes are diverse, the program must reflect that diversity. The assessment procedures as well as the type of information gathered depend on the purpose.

Securing Faculty Involvement

The objective is 100% active involvement of faculty members in every step of the program's evolution. When the program is completed, the faculty must believe the program is theirs, since they had a strong hand in its development. Each discipline may require separate standards and methods, but, for the sake of accuracy and reasonable consistency, they must be reviewed by a higher body, perhaps by the faculty senate, academic dean, or board of trustees. Above all, the faculty must never lose the feeling that they are in control of their destiny.

Seeking Support From Campus Influentials

Every college and university has faculty influentials whose support is mandatory if the evaluation program is to succeed. The support of this handful of faculty heavyweights is needed as the evaluation program is developed or redesigned. Convinced of its worth, these individuals can help bring success to the program. It is practical to court their support and seek their advice.

Seeking Administrative Backing

Administrative support is also vital to the success of the program. No faculty evaluation program can survive without the continuing public support of top-level administrators. They are trained to break logjams, offer acceptable compromises, and lend the force of their office to publicize the program. In addition to being committed to the program and seeing that it operates effectively, administrators must also give the faculty the lead in the program's development and implementation, provide the necessary resources, and support the program with enough enthusiasm to help it overcome week-by-week obstacles.

Collecting Multi-Source Information

To obtain a three-dimensional and reasonably accurate picture of a professor's effectiveness, a number of relevant sources must be consulted (Seldin, 2005). Each information source offers important but limited insight. No single source is enough for tenure, promotion, or

retention decisions. All of them together build a more solid foundation for administrative decisions. *Students* provide an assessment of
teaching skills, content and structure of the course, workload,
teacher-student interactions, clarity of presentation, and student
advising. *Faculty peers* provide a review of teaching materials, mastery
and currency of subject matter, original research, professional recognition, participation in the academic community, interest in and concern for teaching, research/publication, and service to the nonacademic community. *Administrators* provide an appraisal of the workload
and other teaching responsibilities, student course enrollment, service
to the institution, and teaching improvement. *Professors* provide self-
appraisals as teachers, student advisors, researchers, and members of
the academic and nonacademic communities.

Experience suggests that in addition to multiple sources, successful evaluation programs also use multiple methods to obtain
information on faculty performance. Among the more popular
methods are ratings and surveys, classroom observation and videotaping, and written evaluations of research/publication contributions by on- and off-campus personnel. In practice, the number of
methods used is limited by time, cost, and magnitude of the decision.

Selecting the Evaluation Instruments

Starting from scratch to develop a faculty evaluation program is to
reinvent the wheel. A wide range of programs operate with varying
degrees of success at institutions all over the country. An institution
looking for a program would be prudent to adapt—not adopt—an
existing program by tailoring it to local needs, local politics, and
local traditions.

Using Local Expertise

Many colleges and universities can tap their own on-campus expertise in professors trained in test construction, research design, and
statistical methods. Such faculty can shape the questionnaires and

forms and structure appropriate methods of data analysis. If needed, specialists from other institutions, more experienced in handling the sometimes tricky adaptation of an evaluation program, can augment on-campus expertise.

Discussing Expectations

Each professor must be aware of program expectations. He or she should meet with the department chair yearly to discuss what constitutes satisfactory and exemplary performance. The meeting should yield agreement on the criteria, and their weights, for the professor's evaluation. The agreement should be consistent with institutional and departmental goals, and it should include the yardsticks that will show how the professor fared in meeting the agreed-upon performance standards.

Training the Evaluators

Professors often find themselves in alien territory when asked to appraise their colleagues' performance. For this task they need training, or at least a few orientation sessions. At a minimum, professors should be taught:

- What to look for
- How to use the evaluation instruments
- How to work together with other evaluators
- How results will be used
- How faculty evaluation leads to faculty development
- Recent research findings on faculty evaluation

Such training is best conducted by faculty colleagues on campus who are highly respected for their solid knowledge of the particular program and faculty evaluation in general.

Administering the Rating Forms

No matter how good the forms and how open the communication, faulty administration can wreck the program. With this in mind, specific characteristics must be included to assure the program a decent chance of success. There must be:

- A regular rating schedule
- Clear and consistent written instructions
- Well-constructed rating forms
- Meaningful standards
- A secure location for storing and processing the rating forms
- A dry run to discover and eliminate bugs in the system

Applying the Evaluation Data

When the purpose of evaluation is to improve performance, the rating forms should be issued to students, faculty colleagues, and the to-be-appraised professor early in the term. Five weeks into the term is suggested. With the rating results in hand, the professor's performance can be monitored and deficiencies corrected.

When the purpose of evaluation is for personnel decisions, the forms should be completed within the last two weeks of the semester. A note of caution: The professor's entire performance, including teaching, research, publication, committee work, and student advising, should be assessed several times over several semesters by several evaluation sources before it is accepted as reliable data. To be avoided is relying on data from one class, one semester, one classroom observation, or one evaluator because it may well do gross injustice to the reality of the professor's performance.

Conclusion

No perfect faculty evaluation system exists today on any college or university campus. It probably never will. Perhaps it is as unrealizable a concept as the perfect human being. But because the system or human being remains imperfect, we cannot justify abandoning it. Many of us have managed to live—and live well—with our imperfections. Clearly, we must continue the efforts to perfection, acknowledging it as an unachievable goal. Every faculty evaluation program needs the kindly ministrations of faculty and administrators to improve it. The goal, therefore, is improvement, not perfection.

BIBLIOGRAPHY

McKeachie, W., & Seldin, P. (2005). *Changing practices in evaluating teaching.* Paper presented at the 30th annual Professional and Organizational Development Network Conference, Milwaukee, WI.

Seldin, P. (2004). *Evaluating and improving faculty performance.* Paper presented at Michigan State University, East Lansing, MI.

Seldin, P. (2005). *Evaluating faculty performance.* Paper presented at the American Council on Education Department Chair Seminar, San Antonio, TX.

Essential Operating Principles and Key Guidelines

2

Peter Seldin

Experience warns that when academic administrators announce their intention to develop a program to evaluate faculty performance, the initial reaction is likely to be negative. In truth, some of the objections may be justified if parts of the evaluation program are fuzzy or if faculty are only minimally involved in developing the program. Too many evaluation programs overlook the familiar epigram "It's not whether you win or lose but how you play the game." Sharp differences of opinion may arise over a definition of the word "performance." *Which* kinds of performance should be appraised? *How* should the evaluation be conducted? *Who* should participate? *How* should the results be obtained?

The development of any systematic method for evaluating faculty performance is a time-consuming and complex process. But the demand for improvement of evaluation programs is getting louder. No one seriously believes, however, that improvement of evaluation programs will cure all the ills of higher education. Evaluation is a tool for the collection of information. It is not an end in itself. Human judgment determines whether the information is used correctly or incorrectly. Misused, evaluation can be destructive. Used properly, it can be an instrument of change.

Essential Operating Principles

Because colleges and universities differ widely and serve various constituencies, an effective faculty evaluation program should follow certain basic operating principles.

- *The institution's frame of reference.* The institution's history, purpose, needs, and stage of development should be the backdrop for the assessment of faculty performance. For example, the frame of reference for a 200-year-old research university is worlds apart from that of a 25-year-old liberal arts college.

- *Multipurpose.* Given the differences in institutional purposes, the faculty evaluation program should be tailored to the needs of the faculty being evaluated, as well as the campus administrators and the institution as a whole.

- *Multifaceted.* To be fair and complete, the evaluation should cover a wide range of faculty activities and responsibilities, weighted according to importance.

- *Multi-methods.* To obtain a more accurate and in-depth picture of overall faculty performance, a wide range of sources should be used for data collection.

Key Guidelines for the Psychological Process of Evaluation

A good place to begin when developing or revising a faculty evaluation program is to consider certain elements of the psychological process.

Process Is at Least as Important as Product

In truth, it takes less time to touch bases than it does to mend fences. Evaluation systems are produced by people and therefore reflect their strengths, weaknesses, hopes, fears, and desire to be consulted in determining how things will be done that affect them.

Willingness to Change Is Inversely Proportional to Proximity

For many people, it is easier to speak about needed reforms in Africa, in a nearby university, or even in another academic department, than to address the situation that affects one directly. Most of us have two voices. One says, "There must be a better way." The other says, "Hold on to what is known and familiar, even if it's not good." Most academics (and most nonacademics, too) resist change. Given this situation, how can change be nudged forward? The answer probably lies in a combination of appeals to professionalism, self-interest, pride, and the use of *gentle* pressure.

Expect Resistance

Take into account the tendency that professors share with most human beings to regard evaluation as an implicit threat. This natural resistance must be nullified by genuine understanding and by pointing out the numerous advantages of objective, fact-based administrative personnel decisions. It is a much more effective approach than to flex administrative muscle, which, instead of ending faculty resistance, simply drives it underground. To soften faculty resistance, experience suggests that sufficient time—a year or even two years—should be allowed for acceptance and implementation. The evaluation system should be viewed as experimental and not etched in stone.

Keep Strategy Flexible and Low-Key

The faculty evaluation process and procedures being developed must be tailored to the uniqueness of a particular campus or department. Discussing strategy in the abstract may be useful if it generates creative ideas and approaches but ultimately it must specifically address what should be done, how the objectives should be accomplished, who should be involved, and what timetable should be used. Both a flexible strategy and a low-key approach to developing it are recommended.

Allow for Individual Differences

It is wise to allow room for individual differences in the development of evaluation criteria, as long as these differences can be tolerated by the institution. The criteria used to evaluate an instructor will be somewhat different from those used to evaluate a full professor. Too often, colleges and universities center attention on the fine points of methodology rather than on criteria. For example, they spend more time deciding which week student rating forms will be distributed than discussing what students will evaluate.

Build in Several Review Levels and a Clearly Defined Appeals Process

These procedural safeguards will detect errors of fact and interpretation and will instill confidence in the integrity of the faculty evaluation program.

Evaluate the Faculty Evaluation Program From Time to Time

The evaluation program must include an internal feedback mechanism for the purpose of regular review. It is comforting to faculty members to know that the evaluation process, itself, is steadily undergoing review and possible unfair elements are being corrected. It is essential that the mechanics of the review be spelled out in advance and in detail. A periodic assessment of the entire evaluation program is necessary as a basic safeguard.

Key Guidelines for the General Process of Evaluation

By now, virtually every college and university has constructed some sort of faculty evaluation program. Unfortunately, in the rush to judgments, some of the patchwork constructions relied on faulty data-gathering methods and poorly devised rating instruments. But other institutions developed faculty evaluation programs that worked well. They successfully separated the faculty wheat from the chaff. What are the benchmarks of such programs?

- There must be a clear linkage between the evaluation program and academic rewards. If the process produces only negative consequences, it is inviting failure. What good is a system that produces only faculty resentment and discredits itself?

- The evaluation program must be presented in a candid, complete, and accurate way to every faculty member. Any sugarcoating or obfuscation in the explanatory process or in the implementation of the program may doom it from the start. The goal is for the entire faculty to know—clearly, accurately, and completely—the precise requirements and evidence needed for decisions about retention, salary increases, promotion, and tenure.

- The evaluation program should be based on the idea that the purpose of gathering quantified, objective data is to shape a subjective decision. The data form the conduit for the judgment, the means to an end. Yet caution must be exercised about the extent of human judgment in the program, since human judgment divorced from objective data may be an invitation to tyranny. Perhaps the best program is one that blends objective data into subjective decisions.

- The evaluation policies and procedures must be in accordance with established civil rights guidelines and affirmative action clauses. In today's legal environment, it is the lucky institution that escapes lawsuits by aggrieved professors who believe they have been denied tenure, promotion, or contract renewal for discriminatory reasons. Many evaluation programs have been challenged in court as inadequate or biased. Certain data-gathering methods have been found wanting and, in some court decisions, illegal. It is critically important, therefore, for institutions to shore up inadequacies and erase inequities in their faculty evaluation programs before the courts order the changes.

- The primary purpose of the evaluation procedure should be to improve quality of faculty performance, and its approach should be positive rather than punitive. The evaluation procedure should be based on the solid belief that each faculty member possesses different abilities and skills, and that the effort should be on maintaining the strengths and shoring up the weaknesses of faculty.

- If the evaluation system is to be accepted, the faculty must have a strong hand in its development. Each discipline may require separate standards and methods, but for accuracy's sake they must be reviewed by a higher body, perhaps by the faculty senate or academic dean. Above all, the faculty must be directly involved with developing and running the program. They must never lose the feeling that they are in control of their destiny.

- Starting from zero to develop a faculty evaluation program is to reinvent the wheel. Many programs operate with success around the country. An institution desiring a program would be prudent to adapt—not adopt—an existing program by tailoring it to meet local needs, politics, or traditions. The evaluation instruments and procedures must be firmly rooted in the purposes and academic culture of the particular college or university.

- All faculty members must know the performance standards by which they will be evaluated. Specifically, they must know what constitutes exemplary, satisfactory, and unsatisfactory performance. Additionally, they must know what criteria and weights will be used for their evaluation. Should a faculty member fall short of the fixed standards, that failure should be discussed with him or her far in advance of a termination decision. Faculty should be given every opportunity to grow in ways that will benefit both the individual and the institution.

- Deciding *what* to evaluate is one of the most difficult problems in developing a performance evaluation system. Small wonder that evaluating a faculty member's performance can be perplexing when one considers how quickly a football fan concludes that a team's quarterback is a poor player because several of his passes have been intercepted. An objective appraisal would raise the following questions:

  ~ Were the passes really bad or did the receivers run the wrong patterns?

  ~ Did the offensive line give the quarterback adequate protection?

  ~ Did he call those plays himself, or were they sent in by the coach?

  ~ Was the quarterback recovering from an injury?

  ~ How good is the vision of the fan?

  ~ Did he or she have a good view of the television through the room's smoky haze?

  ~ Was the fan talking with a friend during the game?

  ~ How many beers did the fan drink during the game?

  In comparison with a barroom judgment of a quarterback's performance, the evaluation of a faculty member is considerably more complex and consequential.

- To obtain a three-dimensional and reasonably accurate picture of a professor's effectiveness, a number of relevant sources must be consulted. Each information source offers important but limited insight. No single source is enough for tenure, promotion, or retention decisions. All of them together build a more solid foundation for administrative decisions. Truth is not simple. To get at it requires all the help one can muster. Students, faculty peers, administrators, faculty colleagues at other institutions, alumni, and faculty self-appraisal can each provide unique insight. It is imperative to obtain multi-source information to avoid false impressions of the faculty member.

- The evaluation instruments and procedures must provide reliable and valid data that are comparable within and across academic units. The data must be of proper technical level and quality to be trustworthy and used exclusively for the intended purpose. The program must be careful to eliminate such critical defects as an irregular rating schedule, bias resulting from flawed instructions, and inconsistent or inadequate standards.

- If it is to be effective, the faculty evaluation system must be accepted by those who evaluate and those who are evaluated. Individuals who do not endorse the system, or do so reluctantly, are unlikely to respond thoughtfully and meaningfully when asked to supply assessment data. Nor are faculty likely to respond with any enthusiasm to performance feedback when they perceive their evaluations as less than fair and accurate.

- The faculty evaluation policies and practices must have the active support of top-level academic administrators. They must be publicly committed to the program, see that it operates effectively, and provide the necessary human and financial resources.

- Every evaluation program whose results apply to tenure, promotion, or retention decisions must include a grievance mechanism. It is wise to set up two committees, one to hear procedural and the other substantive grievances. The grievance procedures must be detailed in advance as part of the faculty evaluation program. An appellate procedure must be available. Since group decisions are generally more acceptable, the committee's decision should be appealed to the faculty senate or the board of trustees rather than to the president or academic vice president.

- Many faculty evaluation programs falter because of defective administrative machinery. The most prevalent defects include an irregular rating schedule, bias resulting from flawed instructions, inconsistent or inadequate standards, and poorly constructed rating forms. A suggested first step is a dry run to gain needed experience in the construction and administration of rating forms. The dry run has the added advantage of stimulating faculty and administrative thinking about the content of the forms so that suggestions for desirable modifications can be made. In the shakedown, unforeseen problems can be corrected. The experience adds substantially to the success potential of the evaluation program.

- Many faculty find themselves in alien territory when asked to evaluate their colleagues' performance. For this task they need training, or at least a few orientation sessions. It is axiomatic that the better the training, the better the evaluators. Thus faculty should be taught:

  ~ What to look for

  ~ How to use the evaluation instruments

  ~ How to work together with other evaluators

  ~ How results will be used

  ~ How faculty evaluation leads to faculty development

  ~ The function and responsibilities of the evaluators

  ~ Recent research findings on faculty evaluation

  ~ The mechanics of the program

  ~ How faculty evaluation is part of the institution's comprehensive evaluation of deans, chairs, and other administrators

  Training of evaluators is best done on campus by colleagues highly respected for their solid knowledge of the particular program on the campus and faculty evaluation in general.

- There is a danger of evaluation overkill. If the faculty evaluation program requires a formal appraisal of a professor's performance every semester, or even every year, the quality of feedback will probably decline.

- The cost of implementing and maintaining an evaluation program must be weighed from time to time against the benefits of the program. Just getting a system started takes many hours of developmental costs. Also, the time involved in completing evaluation forms, maintaining appropriate records, communicating with various sources of evaluation information and the faculty being evaluated, and working with individual faculty members on developmental activities is considerable. But the benefits of an effective evaluation program will far outweigh its costs. Promotion, tenure, and retention decisions are made easier because they rest on documented job performance. Best of all, the rising level of faculty performance benefits the institution and the faculty members themselves.

Deficiencies in Evaluation Programs

Colleges and universities embarking on a faculty evaluation program or further developing an existing program can avoid many mistakes by learning from the experience of other institutions. There is no special virtue in repeating errors. The following deficiencies are common in faculty evaluation programs:

- Faculty are expected to turn in perfect performance in every area.
- Programs are not rooted in the traditions, goals, and style of the college or university.
- Unfair evaluations of good faculty.
- Vague criteria for administrative judgments leave individuals in the dark about the performance expected of them.
- Excessive cost in time and energy.
- An unwillingness to confront less effective faculty with realistic ratings.
- The entire evaluation is based on information from just one source.
- Excessive time is demanded of individuals involved in the evaluation process.

- Assessment criteria and procedures are not clear or unilaterally selected.
- Evaluation policies and/or procedures violate civil rights guidelines.
- Inadequate data on teaching, research, and service, the three major areas of faculty work.
- Confidentiality of results is not maintained and distribution of results is not controlled.
- Negative feedback is delivered without skill, leaving the faculty member demoralized.
- Performance is not compared to the previously determined standards.
- Inconsistent ratings by individuals in different units of the same institution.
- Resistance to the evaluation program because of its preconceived inability to make fair judgments or because the system is seen as defective.
- A delay in feedback to faculty, thereby delaying effective reinforcement.
- Insufficient time is allowed for implementation of the program.
- Institutional failure to pay sufficient attention to faculty development programs, expecting the evaluation process by itself to solve performance problems.

Important Precautions

When developing or upgrading faculty evaluation forms and procedures, experience suggests the following precautions:

- Avoid evaluations by individuals not competent to make them.
- Avoid evaluation instruments issued by special-interest groups.

- Avoid overstressing individual items apart from the context of the entire evaluation instrument.

- Avoid accepting evaluation as a power play in collective bargaining.

- Avoid the mass distribution of evaluation results.

- Avoid assigning the same value to different evaluations—consider the background of each individual or group responding.

- Avoid developing evaluation instruments and procedures during an academic crisis.

- Avoid making final recommendations based on evaluation materials that represent only a part of the total picture.

Improving Faculty Evaluation Programs: A Composite Summary

I have served as consultant to scores of colleges and universities eager to improve their faculty evaluation programs. What follows is a composite summary of their institutional experience.

Our college came to the project with a loosely applied faculty evaluation system. For the evaluation of teaching, student ratings were our only source of information. For the evaluation of research, we looked at a list of publications but, because of time pressures, we didn't actually read any of them. For the evaluation of service, we just scanned a list of committees. We filled out evaluation forms, but most people weren't sure if they were used on an institution-wide basis.

Our first impulse was to develop new forms right away. If student ratings were to be used, why not get started on finding the right form with the right questions? Same thing with forms to evaluate research and service. Fortunately, this tendency soon gave way to a realization that consensus about purpose had to be developed first if the changes were to be meaningful. We then expanded our original committee with the new appointees coming from academic units not represented by the original members.

Then we met with the provost. He told us of his administrative needs, gave us broad parameters, told us to work out the specifics of the evaluation program, and said—provided we came up with a program that was within his broad parameters— he would provide financial and human support for whatever program we developed.

We also met with the director of human resources. She told us about the current civil rights legislation together with affirmative action clauses, shared with us examples of evaluation procedures that have been found inadequate or biased by the courts, and offered the assistance of her office as we moved forward.

Our next task was to conduct a campus-wide survey of faculty. The questionnaire asked for reactions to the current evaluation system, feedback on what was needed to improve it, and questions about attitude toward using certain techniques such as videotaping teaching. We received a 72% response rate.

We carefully reviewed the faculty survey results. Their feedback was invaluable. Also, we reviewed the current literature on faculty evaluation and visited several colleges and universities in our area to discuss their faculty evaluation programs. All of this took several months. It wasn't until six months after we began that we were able to propose an initial blueprint to the faculty. The entire evaluation committee attended each of the three open hearings that followed. Those hearings led to some modification in the proposed evaluation procedures and forms. Our approach was marked by patience and a willingness to compromise.

The revised faculty evaluation program included five sections:

1) A statement of purpose
2) A definition of the kinds of activities that would be evaluated
3) Sources of information
4) What would be asked of each of these sources
5) How the information would be used

Endorsement by the faculty, provost, and vice president for human resources followed. Only then did we take on the development of evaluation forms and specific procedures. About one year after beginning, we were given the go-ahead for a dry run to gain experience and locate and correct program weaknesses. We expect that it will take about two years for acceptance and implementation.

Conclusion

Despite much progress in faculty evaluation, the bad news is that there is still no simple way to assess performance. The notion of a precise method of appraisal is certainly appealing, but it is highly unlikely that a way will ever be found to measure the multidimensional performance of faculty with one yardstick. The kernel of good news, however, is that much of the concern about evaluation formats and rating instruments seems to have been unwarranted.

If anything has been learned, it is that there is no single "correct" way to evaluate faculty performance in teaching, research, or service. There are many ways. Colleges and universities should experiment to find the method that feels "right" to them. Reviewing the literature on faculty evaluation can help (e.g., Arreola, 2000; Buller, 2004; Groth, 2004; Seldin, 2004; Sorenson & Johnson, 2003). So can talking with colleagues at other institutions. But in the end, what feels right at a particular college or university will likely emerge from extensive discussion and compromise.

REFERENCES

Arreola, R. A. (2000). *Developing a comprehensive faculty evaluation system: A handbook for college faculty and administrators on designing and operating a comprehensive faculty evaluation system* (2nd ed.). Bolton, MA: Anker.

Buller, J. L. (2004, Winter). Tips for conducting effective faculty evaluation sessions. *The Department Chair, 14*(3), 5–8.

Groth, M. (2004, Fall). What do students want from us? *The Department Chair, 15*(2), 15–17.

Seldin, P. (2004). *The teaching portfolio: A practical guide to improved performance and promotion/tenure decisions* (3rd ed.). Bolton, MA: Anker.

Sorenson, D. L., & Johnson, T. D. (2003). *New directions for teaching and learning: No. 96. Online student ratings of instruction.* San Francisco, CA: Jossey-Bass.

Building a Climate for Faculty Evaluation That Improves Teaching

3

Mary Lou Higgerson

Assessing faculty performance in teaching yields information that is essential to enhancing student learning, faculty development, program quality, and institutional success. Although such assessment is not new, current demands give performance review a new shape and purpose. An example may help to illustrate this change. At one time, a peer review of teaching might have read:

> Professor Smith demonstrated a fine command of the subject. His lecture was well organized and clear. His effective use of visual aids helped to reinforce the major points of the lecture. My observation of Professor Smith's teaching suggests that he is an excellent instructor.

This review says nothing about student learning. Today, this evaluative statement might prompt concern about Professor Smith's effectiveness because it offers no evidence that the instructor has engaged students in learning. When the focus is on student learning, a positive peer review statement might read:

> Professor Smith engaged the students in learning by using a real-world case study that permitted them to discover the complexity of the constructs being studied. The class, as taught, generated considerable student interest in the subject and the assignment challenged all students to pursue their interest in the topic independently.

When the focus is on student learning, the assessment of teaching takes into account what students are doing because it is assumed that they are active participants who are engaged in learning.

Both the focus and expectation for teaching evaluation have changed. New and different indicators of teaching effectiveness demand that we revise our approach to assessing instruction. This chapter describes how to do this in a way that builds a climate that improves teaching. While the strategies presented would help enhance performance in all areas of faculty work, the discussion will focus on improving teaching to permit a more detailed discussion of each strategy.

Strategies for Building a Climate
That Improves Teaching

The strategies presented can be implemented in a single department or across the entire campus. All of them involve shaping the communication about teaching evaluation in a way that reduces faculty resistance to being reviewed and optimizes the benefit for individual faculty, students, and the institution. The strategies can and should be modified to accommodate conditions unique to a specific department or campus.

Reconceptualize the Task

When faculty value the information obtained through performance evaluation, the process is more comfortable and beneficial for all involved. It is also more likely to yield tangible improvements. However, chairs and deans find that faculty can be resistant or indifferent to evaluation. It is important that faculty perceive teaching evaluation as an activity that supports professional development and enhances teaching success.

The first strategy is to reconceptualize the activity of evaluating teaching in a way that makes it more appealing to faculty. This can be done by changing how participants talk about the activity of assessing "teaching." Intentionally refer to performance *counseling* instead of performance *evaluation*. Such a shift in word choice is more than semantics. It can alter how the participants perceive and respond to the activity. The word *evaluation* suggests a critical dimension whereas the word *counseling* is a broader construct that encompasses both assessment and coaching. How faculty think about the activity will influence the process and the outcome. If the focus is on performance counseling, the activity is collaborative and the shared objective is to enhance success.

Reconceptualizing the task from evaluation to counseling accrues two additional benefits worth mentioning. First, it makes the activity of assessing faculty performance more comfortable for those persons conducting the review because they can assume the role of professional coach and shed the less comfortable role of judge or critic. When the process is more comfortable, faculty are less resistant and defensive, so it is possible to optimize the review outcome. Second, the focus on performance counseling (instead of performance evaluation) reduces the potential for conflict because coaching places both the reviewer and the faculty member being reviewed on the same team with a common purpose—to improve faculty performance and thereby enhance faculty success.

To illustrate the difference between performance evaluation and performance counseling, consider the example of the chair who must work with an untenured faculty member on teaching improvement. Assume that student evaluations indicate that students find the course objectives unclear (see Chapter 4). In a teaching evaluation session, the student evaluations would be reviewed and discussed as "concerns to address." The faculty member is likely to interpret the "concerns" discussed as negative judgments of his or her effectiveness in the classroom. In a more traditional teaching evaluation session, a chair might comment as follows:

In reviewing student evaluations for your courses, I noticed that students believe the course objectives are unclear. This finding is fairly consistent across all course subjects and levels. Consequently, it will be important for you to give more attention to making the course objectives clear for students. Paying more attention to this aspect of your teaching will likely improve your student evaluations across the board.

Upon hearing this the faculty member might become defensive, and a defensive posture does not support honest reflection, which is the first step toward improved performance. Moreover, while the evaluative comment makes clear the expected outcome, it offers no guidance for how to achieve the desired result.

The same findings, however, presented in a session that is focused on counseling teaching improvement can produce a very different discussion and outcome. The focus moves from describing the finding to strategizing with the individual faculty member about ways in which to respond to the students' perception. The person conducting the performance counseling is more likely to describe the ways in which the learning objectives for the course might be highlighted for students and the shared objective to improve teaching is more apparent. In using a performance counseling approach, a chair's comment to the individual faculty member would be more in line with the following:

Student response on the standardized survey instrument suggests that they are not grasping with sufficient clarity the learning objectives for the course. How are you currently informing students of the learning objectives for each course? [Discussion would follow.] Have you given any thought to what you might do to make this aspect of your teaching more prominent for students? [Discussion would follow.] In my own teaching, for example, I have found that it can be helpful to refer students back to that portion of the syllabus where the learning objectives are stated. I find that this strategy also serves as a mini midterm assessment of where we are while we have an opportunity to revisit some material if students believe we have not sufficiently covered a particular learning objective. Can you envision trying something like this? [Wait for reflection and reply and listen carefully.]

This approach to performance review is less likely to evoke a defensive response from the faculty member and offers specific guidance on how to achieve the desired outcome.

The difference between the two examples illustrates the change that can occur when one shifts from performance *evaluation* to performance *counseling*. In performance counseling, the communication is less judgmental and invites the faculty member to engage in the conversation in a way that reinforces the purpose—to improve the individual faculty member's performance and enhance his or her prospects for success. Reconceptualizing performance review creates a climate that improves teaching because faculty are more likely to perceive the value of performance counseling as a means to enhancing their chances to succeed.

Make Teaching a Priority

Institutional policy may prescribe that department chairs conduct an annual evaluation of faculty performance. Although such policies are intended to ensure that faculty performance is reviewed on a regular basis, the stipulation that review be conducted annually can actually diminish the attention paid to faculty performance. Conducted on an annual basis, performance review becomes a task to complete once a year and not an integral part of the department values or daily activity. To create a climate that improves teaching, it is necessary to make teaching an institutional priority. When faculty recognize that student learning is important to documenting academic and institutional quality, they will be better able to understand how their teaching constitutes the core of what the institution promises to students.

When teaching is a campus priority, the need to assess and improve teaching becomes more apparent as critical to institutional success.

Consider, for example, the dynamic at a large doctoral-granting institution that recently launched a public relations campaign to articulate the attention paid to instruction at the undergraduate level. Faculty at the institution may believe that teaching takes second place to research activity because traditionally more attention has been paid to research, scholarly publications, and grant activity than to teaching. Until faculty understand that teaching undergraduate students is an institutional priority, efforts to impose performance counseling that is directed toward improving teaching for undergraduate students will likely be resisted, if not resented. Yet the institution will only be able to deliver on its promise to undergraduate students if faculty understand and accept that teaching undergraduate students is a priority that is as important as research activity. Saying it on campus is not enough. The administration needs to reinforce the institutional value placed on teaching undergraduate students in every action including, for example, the assessment of tenure and promotion applications, support for faculty development, and the allocation of resources. By linking the subject of performance evaluation to institutional priorities in a credible way, it is possible to make faculty teaching performance a campus-wide priority and build an expectation for continuous counseling that is essential to institutional success.

Create a Context That Is Faculty-Centered

Faculty are more accepting of performance counseling when they perceive a personal benefit. It can be helpful, for example, to subsume the assessment of teaching as part of a larger program geared toward the faculty member's professional development and/or successful bid for tenure or promotion. Few faculty will resist counseling designed to enhance their quest for professional advancement on the campus or within the discipline. When faculty believe that they benefit personally from performance counseling, they become willing participants in the assessment of their teaching because they perceive the process as one that enhances their own ability to succeed.

Consider, for example, a campus that does not have a post-tenure review policy. A top-down mandate calling for post-tenure review could produce considerable resistance whereas a proactive plan for investing in faculty development (tenured and untenured) for the purpose of enhancing individual and collective success in teaching today's students could be well received. When the context for performance counseling is faculty-centered, the language and approach to the individual counseling session reveals an investment in the individual faculty member's success. Consider the following evaluative statement made by a department chair during a performance counseling session: "It is important that students feel engaged in the subject and the course." This statement offers a student-centered evaluative comment regarding teaching. While it signals a performance expectation, it implies that the faculty member is expected to teach in a way that satisfies student expectations. Even the faculty member who works hard at teaching and is committed to teaching well might be unmoved or discouraged by such an appeal. As worded, the evaluative statement makes how students "feel" in a class the institutional objective. Further, it implies that students determine their level of engagement and, in doing so, passes the responsibility for effective teaching to students.

It is possible to build a climate that improves teaching by creating a faculty-centered context for performance counseling. When evaluative statements are cast in a faculty-centered context, they evoke a more positive response from faculty. Consider the potential difference in a faculty member's reaction if the previous statement made by a department chair is recast as follows:

> This is a tough subject to teach. I know you have a lot of content to cover, but student evaluations of the course suggest that students

believe they are unable to master the material presented through lecture in ways that permit them to work with the concepts.

This statement makes no implication about the faculty member being deficient or unable to review his or her teaching, but frames the task as one of educating today's students. Further, it leaves open the possibility that students may not be taking full advantage of assignments or class activities that are designed to engage them in the subject. The statement, however, reinforces that the faculty member has ultimate control and responsibility for teaching effectiveness.

Faculty-centered performance counseling minimizes the likelihood that faculty will resist or resent counseling. A faculty-centered context reduces defensiveness, thereby increasing the likelihood that faculty will be more receptive to coaching that improves teaching.

Be Concrete and Specific in Setting Performance Expectations

It is important that performance expectations are stated in concrete, behavioral terms. Institutional policy seldom offers such clarity. For example, institutional policy might discuss the need to demonstrate "effective teaching" in a tenure or promotion application without ever operationalizing what effective teaching looks like. When performance expectations are not clear in behavioral terms, faculty are more apt to misunderstand them or develop their own performance expectations. Ambiguity about performance expectations undermines the climate for performance counseling because it can be demoralizing and discouraging to work hard without achieving positive recognition or results (see Chapter 10).

Faculty hold perceptions of students and teaching that may or may not be consistent with the institution's performance expectations. A faculty member may believe that a "dumb" question from a student does not warrant response. The faculty member may conclude that the student asking a "dumb" question did not read the assignment and believe that it would be unfair to other more prepared students to spend valuable class time responding to questions posed by an unprepared student. Such reasoning might prompt a faculty member to be dismissive of some student questions when the campus instructional mission is to do otherwise. When offering evaluative comment regarding someone's teaching, it is important to illustrate the evaluative statements with concrete behavioral examples. To illustrate this principle, assume that students have complained that Professor Smith causes them to "feel stupid and unimportant" when he ignores their questions. Imagine Professor Smith's reaction to the following evaluative statement:

> I am confident that you don't intend to be dismissive of students, but several of the students enrolled in your class report that you make them feel stupid and unimportant. I know that we can count on you to be responsive to their concerns.

The evaluative statement is likely to make Professor Smith defensive. The statement offers no hint of why some students perceive Professor Smith as thinking them "stupid and unimportant." Worse yet, it offers no guidance on how to remedy the situation. It is likely to be of little consequence that the person making the evaluative statement offers assurance that Professor Smith would not intentionally communicate a negative view of students and confidence in Professor Smith's ability to remedy the misunderstanding.

Now consider the probable difference in Professor Smith's reaction when the evaluative comment offers specific, concrete examples as part of the evaluative comment.

> A few of your students paid me a visit yesterday. They described an incident in which one of the students asked a question about theory X. Do you remember that incident? [Wait for reflection and reply.] Apparently, the question asked was one that many held so they were anxious for your reply and hoped that it would help them comprehend theory X. Perhaps because they hoped that your response to the question would clarify their confusion

about theory X, the students perceived your short reply as being dismissive of them. Two students explicitly said that the exchange caused them to "feel stupid and unimportant." I assured the students that this was not your attitude toward them and offered to let you know that those who are still struggling to understand theory X would appreciate a more detailed response to the question.

In this communication, the person making the evaluative statement offers specific information about behavior that produced the student perception. Professor Smith is less likely to become defensive and will likely appreciate the constructive interaction that the individual who is counseling him had with the students when they waged their complaint. Better still, Professor Smith knows precisely what to do to remedy the misunderstanding, and by doing so, Professor Smith can improve student learning.

Unless the evaluative statements are linked to concrete behaviors, it is only criticism and not a strategy for improvement. Similarly, when a faculty member promises to work harder or to get better at teaching, it is important to delineate what concrete behaviors will represent working harder and likely lead to improvement. Until such abstract goal statements are linked to concrete behaviors, they represent only good intent and not a tangible plan for improvement.

Practical advice wears well and is more faculty-friendly when it is immediately useful. Without practical suggestions, faculty are more likely to hear evaluative comments as criticism. Without clear and concrete performance expectations, faculty can work hard and still fail to satisfy expectations or realize teaching improvement. By describing performance expectation in concrete and specific behavioral terms, it is possible to generate specific strategies that will more likely produce successful outcomes.

Establish Expectations for Continuous Review

When the counseling of teaching improvement becomes a year-round activity rather than a yearly event, it is possible to reduce anxiety that may occur with more formal teaching evaluations. It also helps to establish a climate in which offering constructive comments for teaching improvement is a normal everyday occurrence because teaching improvement is a core value in the department and on the campus. It is possible to establish expectations for continuous review by using informal communication to recognize progress and offer comment on what is going well and what might be done differently. The more informal the constructive comments are, the easier it is to maintain the coaching perspective of teaching assessment. As educators, we understand that evaluative comments are more meaningful and are therefore more likely to result in improved performance when they are offered close to the event or when the observation is fresh. Further, the more informal and frequent evaluative statements are made about teaching, the more peers will engage in offering constructive comments to each other. By encompassing both formal and informal communication in performance counseling, it is possible to create a climate that improves teaching because constructive comments are frequent and better received.

Minimize the Potential for Conflict

It is natural for people to become defensive when they believe that they or their work is the subject of criticism. By moving to a coaching or counseling role, it is possible to minimize the potential for conflict. It is also essential to depersonalize the discussion of faculty performance. Consider the difference between the following two statements:

> *Statement A*: You are dismissive of students who appear less interested in the subject.

Statement B: Students are more likely to have an interest in the subject when they recognize that you perceive them as able to master the material being studied.

The first statement labels the faculty member in a less than flattering way. The second statement describes a specific behavior that would be more successful with students. In providing a behavioral example of what might work, the person offering the evaluative comment implies that the faculty member can effectively implement this piece of coaching. In Statement A, the evaluative comment is offered as a conclusion about the faculty member's perspective and approach. It labels the faculty member in an unflattering way, which will likely cause a defensive response. Statement A, therefore, contains no hint that the person making it believes that the faculty member can change or improve this aspect of his or her teaching. In reviewing these two statements, we can easily understand how Statement A would more likely evoke a defensive reaction than would Statement B. When people become defensive during a review, the opportunity for real growth and teaching improvement is lost to time spent defending one's approach and merit. Individuals also tend to hear evaluative comments as criticism rather than as suggestions for enhancing success. To create a climate that improves teaching, it is important to eliminate unnecessary defensiveness and minimize the potential for conflict by depersonalizing performance counseling.

Language use is critical when one is trying to minimize the potential for conflict. In addition to discussing behaviors rather than personalities, it is important to select language with full consideration of the other person's perspective. For example, in conducting a performance counseling session of a senior faculty member who is a few years away from retirement, one should not talk about the tremendous potential that person has to become a good teacher. This statement would likely be heard as an insult by a senior faculty member. Instead, it would be more fitting to talk about the legacy that the senior faculty member may wish to leave for less experienced colleagues.

Those conducting performance counseling sessions can minimize the potential for conflict by depersonalizing the activity and by using language that makes clear their confidence in the person's ability to improve. Using language that takes into account the faculty member's perspective will help to create a climate for performance counseling that improves teaching.

Recognize and Support Improvement

We know that students are more likely to sustain efforts toward improvement when faculty acknowledge their efforts and progress. The same holds true when counseling faculty to improve teaching. Beyond personally recognizing efforts to improve, it is possible to celebrate effort and success within the department or across the campus. The celebration of teaching success can take a variety of forms. At Baldwin-Wallace College, we implemented two programs that facilitate campus-wide conversations about pedagogy and also offer an opportunity to celebrate individual teaching success. The first is a Pedagogy Series that entails monthly meetings on a wide range of topics designed to provide faculty with tips and strategies that will be immediately useful. Although we occasionally invite speakers to campus for presentations as part of the series, most of the presentations are made by our own faculty. We might, for example, offer a program on using rubrics and have that program presented by a faculty member who is especially accomplished in the use of rubrics for evaluating and grading students' work. Consequently, the Pedagogy Series is both a vehicle for faculty development and a stage for showcasing the teaching talent we have at the college. It also helps to reinforce that continuous teaching improvement is an institutional priority.

The second program is the Summer Faculty Academy. Each spring faculty are asked to suggest topics for a one-day faculty development program held on the campus. The ideas are collected and faculty are asked through an electronic survey to rate the subjects of greatest interest. The two topics receiving the most votes become two three-hour sessions that fill a one-day program for faculty. Being invited to present at these programs is a way of celebrating excellence because it recognizes in a public forum the talent that resides in our faculty. Presenters can be either tenured or untenured and from any department. Such programs help to fuel the ongoing, campus-wide conversation about pedagogy and, as a result, help to create a climate for continuous performance counseling to improve teaching.

These examples of programs at Baldwin-Wallace College illustrate how structured programs that facilitate faculty development can also serve as a platform for recognizing and celebrating teaching success. Comparable faculty development programs might already be in existence on your campus and can serve these same goals. The strategy is to be intentional in recognizing and supporting teaching improvement.

Closing Summary

The strategies suggested for building a climate for faculty evaluation that improves teaching derive from a common assumption—that performance counseling is essential to improved teaching and we should work to make it a routine and frequent occurrence. Implicit in the strategies is the belief that teaching improvement is no longer a solo venture, but that sustained teaching effectiveness requires the continuous assessment and discussion of pedagogy.

The strategies discussed in this chapter are designed to make performance counseling and teaching improvement dominant threads in the tapestry of academic work. They employ communication that helps to make performance counseling valued by faculty and develops a climate in which the assessment of teaching is commonplace because all recognize the fundamental importance of assessing teaching to improve teaching. The strategies also help to elevate the importance of teaching. When teaching becomes a high priority in the department or on the campus, faculty are more moti-vated to seek and use performance counseling to enhance their teaching success.

There is much that can be gained by building a climate that improves teaching. Any action that results in teaching improvement enhances institutional success. When the climate supports teaching improvement because faculty value the assessment of teaching and performance counseling, there exists tremendous support for the instructional mission of the institution. When the assessment and discussion of pedagogy is commonplace, it is easier to engage both faculty and students in learning.

Uses and Abuses of Student Ratings

4

William Pallett

The use of student ratings of instruction for evaluative purposes is a major issue on many campuses. When a Google™ search of student ratings was conducted in June 2005, over three million citations were reported. Much of this attention occurs because of their influence, sometimes excessive, in personnel evaluation.

Since The IDEA Center is one of the largest providers of a national student ratings system, it is often assumed that we believe student ratings are all that is needed to evaluate teaching effectiveness. This is far from the truth. Our long experience with the student ratings process provides a perspective that reveals both their value and their limitations. This chapter describes the uses of student ratings, identifies abuses that limit their effectiveness, and briefly discusses the additional implications of using an online ratings system.

The Uses of Student Ratings

Student ratings can legitimately serve at least four purposes:

- Formative feedback to improve teaching
- Personnel evaluation
- Program evaluation
- Student advisement

Using Student Ratings to Guide Improvement Efforts

Many institutions say that student ratings are intended to serve formative teaching improvement efforts. A meta-analysis study by Cohen (1980) concludes that real gains in teaching improvement occur when consultative support in interpreting student ratings is provided and used. An academic dean told me a faculty member that he mentored would likely not have obtained tenure if diagnostic information from the IDEA survey had not been available to guide his improvement efforts. Other faculty have told me how valuable student ratings information was in helping them reflect on ways to change teaching approaches to impact student learning.

A careful review of the literature on best teaching practices and student learning is an important step in designing an instrument that will guide teaching improvement (Chickering & Gamson, 1987; Davis, 1993; McKeachie, 2002; Svinicki, 2004; Zull, 2002). If a standard form is used for classes, it is helpful to add questions (either fixed response or open-ended) that are directed at specific topics unique to the class. The information is not only more directly applicable in addressing a specific question, but students have told me they are more thoughtful in their responses since they see it as an indication that the instructor values feedback. I have observed that faculty who tell their students they want and value feedback are more likely to receive information that is truly beneficial.

Regrettably, the diagnostic value of student ratings is often not realized, even though many faculty developers and teaching improvement specialists attest to their potential. There are at least three reasons for this. First, there is so much emphasis on the summative component of student ratings—getting the right number— that what can be learned to improve teaching is often overlooked. This is similar to criticisms of the practice of returning final exams or end-of-semester papers to students with comments to guide their improvement effort; the recommendations often go unread if the grade is acceptable. Second, useful, valid, and reliable student ratings forms are difficult to create. This is especially true in developing a form that can truly support improvement efforts. Third, for real gains in teaching skill to occur, support and mentoring needs to be provided. While those making personnel assessments should not be precluded from guiding improvement efforts, others not involved in the evaluation process also need to be available. A credible mentor is needed to provide feedback and make confidential recommendations. These mentors should be trusted colleagues with excellent teaching reputations who are interpersonally sensitive and genuinely committed to their colleagues' growth and improvement.

Using Student Ratings in Personnel Evaluation

Student ratings are the most frequently used source of evidence for judging teaching effectiveness in the personnel evaluation process (Seldin, 1999). There are many good reasons to include student ratings as a component. The two most important are: 1) students have the greatest opportunity to observe teaching, and 2) they are the intended beneficiaries of that teaching, so it should be of great importance to them. Students are generally skilled at assessing instructor-student rapport and interaction and clarity of communication. They can also provide their perspectives on course difficulty, workload, and grading practices, and self-assess their learning. Such information is relevant to the assessment of teaching effectiveness.

Using Student Ratings for Program Evaluation

Using student ratings as a supplemental source of evidence in the accreditation process or as part of curriculum review is a relatively new phenomenon. Results from individual courses may be combined to create aggregate reports that summarize information about classes from a department, academic program, or general education program. Student ratings instruments whose items focus on specific learning outcomes or teaching methods that are known to support desired learning outcomes are especially helpful.

While aggregate reports are a useful source for providing evidence of teaching effectiveness, their greater value is in supporting continuous improvement efforts. For example, the aggregate report may identify a concern that can be addressed by a group of instructors. The following year, the aggregate report for the same group of classes can be used to assess the success of those targeted improvement efforts. Good assessment programs focus on outcomes as well as on how information is used to guide improvement efforts. Although student ratings instruments need to be revised as we learn more about the teaching-learning process, using the same ratings instrument over time is a useful way of monitoring departmental or course success. Questions such as—Have ratings of learning in the 20-plus sections offered in Psychology 110 increased during the past five years? Are distance sections of this course viewed as positively as face-to-face sections? Have we noticed changes since recent technological improvements were made at our campus?—are illustrative of the kinds of concerns these reports may address.

Obtaining information about general education programs is a place where aggregate reports may be especially useful. With some advanced planning, aggregate reports can be created to assess course outcomes that address specific general education goals.

Another way to use a student ratings instrument in program assessment is through the use of extra questions. Department chairs, deans, and other senior administrators might ask five to ten additional questions that address campus or program concerns or goals that go beyond the specific course. Using this option typically results in obtaining a higher response rate than if a separate survey were administered to focus on these concerns. Campuses using this process tell students that while they may see the extra questions in more than one of their classes they should answer them only once. Another approach that succeeds on campuses that have a high percentage of students (e.g., 80%) enrolled during a specific time period (e.g., 10:00 a.m. on Wednesdays) is to administer the extra questions only during that time. This approach may be helpful in determining whether a more comprehensive survey is needed. For example, if there are concerns about academic advising, asking a question like— Overall, how satisfied have you been with the academic advising you have received?—may prove to be informative. If the instrument does not ask for the student's year in school, ask that as well so that you can receive feedback about advising by student level. If the results are positive, there may be no need to further address an issue. If they are negative, the information from a few items may help you target specific groups of students or specific concerns that merit further attention.

Using Student Ratings for Advisement

The publishing of student ratings information has become more frequent with the advent of the Internet and institutional web sites. The Internet allows for relatively inexpensive deployment and continuous updating of data. Useful information describing a course may be provided to students about the amount of reading, work other than reading, difficulty of subject matter, types of assessment methods used (tests, papers, projects), or how much collaborative work is done. The process becomes problematic when information focuses on an assessment of the teacher rather than on descriptive information about the course and its requirements. When students arrive with preconceived negative expectations about the instructor's teaching ability, judgments about current teaching ability may be unfairly, and unknowingly, influenced by the results of past evaluations.

If a campus opts to provide information about "teacher effectiveness," new instructors should be protected by allowing them to establish a track record before publishing ratings. Waiting two to three years before publishing results seems a fair compromise. By doing that, instructors have an opportunity to use information from student ratings and other sources to hone teaching skills before facing public scrutiny.

Abuses and Misuses of Student Ratings

Until quite recently student ratings have been overemphasized and underutilized. When I joined The IDEA Center in 1997, it was common to learn that a campus relied entirely, or almost entirely, on student ratings to assess teaching effectiveness. When asked if student ratings were used to support teaching improvement efforts, the answer was frequently no. As a consequence, faculty at many institutions saw little or no benefit from student ratings. There was some justifiable fear that one composite number might have an adverse impact on one's professional future, so the stakes were high. New faculty members had made substantial investments of both time and money to get where they were. But most of this preparation was not directed at a major component of their responsibilities—teaching.

While many graduate programs have recently placed greater emphasis on teaching, most of a faculty member's preparation to enter the academy is still focused on acquiring disciplinary knowledge. While such preparation is essential, there is a rapidly expanding body of knowledge about how people learn and the uses of technology to support learning that have typically received little attention in graduate school. Therefore, much of what is important to teaching and learning must be learned on the job. It should not be surprising that initial feedback from student ratings is often discouraging.

By the end of their graduate school experience, new faculty have usually received substantial positive feedback from credible and credentialed graduate professors. When students, whose credibility is suspect, provide negative feedback to them, it is understandable that the results create defensiveness and skepticism. When initial experiences with student ratings are negative and there is no confirmatory evidence from more trusted sources, the value of student ratings will often be challenged. The credibility of any process requires trust. One of the best ways to establish trust is to gather and use information appropriately.

Student ratings are neither inherently good nor bad. How they are used determines their value (see Chapter 3). When they are used well, they can be helpful in supporting the agendas for which they are intended. When abused, trust is lost, impact is negative, and something potentially valuable becomes damaging. Examples of how the value of student ratings may be diminished or lost follow.

Abuse 1: Overreliance on Student Ratings in the Evaluation of Teaching

The IDEA Center has long recommended that student ratings comprise no more than 30% to 50% of the evaluation of teaching (Hoyt & Pallett, 1999). There are a number of components of effective teaching that students are simply *not* well equipped to judge, including:

- The appropriateness of an instructor's objectives
- The instructor's knowledge of the subject matter
- The degree to which instructional processes or materials are current, balanced, and relevant to objectives
- The quality and appropriateness of assessment methods
- The appropriateness of grading standards
- The instructor's support for department teaching efforts such as curriculum development and mentoring new faculty
- The instructor's contribution to a department climate that values teaching

Faculty peers (either local or at a distance) and department/division chairs are much better equipped to address such issues.

No method used to assess teaching effectiveness is perfectly valid, including student ratings. Because personnel decisions dramatically impact both an individual's personal and professional future and the quality of the educational experience an institution provides, it is vital to use multiple sources of information in assessing all components of effective teaching.

Abuse 2: Making Too Much of Too Little

While there is substantial evidence that student ratings are reliable, there is always some "noise" in survey data (see Chapter 10). Therefore, if the same student rating survey was administered two days in a row, results would not be precisely the same. Too often, student ratings averages are treated in the same way as things like height and weight that have much less variability over short time intervals. This problem is exacerbated when there are small numbers of raters making judgments, as is the case in classes with fewer than 10 students.

Campus officials often arrive at judgments that make too much of too little. Is there really a difference between the student ratings averages of 4.0 and 4.1? Differences in salary increase and other personnel recommendations have often been made based on very small differences such as these. To avoid the error of cutting a log with a razor, student ratings results should be categorized into three to five groups for example, "Outstanding," "Exceeds Expectations," "Meets Expectations," "Needs Improvement but Making Progress," and "Fails to Meet Expectations." Utilizing more than three to five groups will almost certainly exceed the measurement sophistication of the instrument being used.

Abuse 3: Not Enough Information to Make an
Accurate Judgment

The IDEA Center recommends ratings of six to eight classes representing all of one's teaching responsibilities be used in the evaluation process—more (eight to twelve) if class sizes are small. At times people infer from this statement that we recommend rating every class every term, which is not the case. Survey fatigue, a consequence of administering too many surveys in a term, can be an abuse unless those completing the forms are fully committed to the process. A better plan is to rate every class once every three years. For example, classes rated in year one should be rated again in year four.

Given the kind of impact personnel decisions have, both on individual faculty and the institution, it is imperative to collect enough information to inform good judgments. For important decisions such as tenure, promotion, or reappointment, using ratings from only a few classes is not appropriate.

Abuse 4: Questionable Administrative Procedures

If student ratings are taken seriously by faculty and administrators, it is likely that students will take them seriously as well. In a meeting with students during a recent campus visit, I asked students how conscientious they were in completing the rating form. Their response was—"It depends." They said if the instructor took the process seriously, they did as well. They cited an example where their ratings were made carefully and thoughtfully. A student cited a department that was especially careful and conscientious in the administration of student ratings; faculty told students how important their feedback was to improving teaching and the curriculum and described how past feedback had been used to make improvements. In contrast, the students reported that a tenured faculty member in another department said he had no interest in what they said. In fact, he told them he rarely looked at the results when they were returned to him. Student reaction was predictable—"Why should I care if he doesn't?"

During a campus visit I heard faculty tell how a colleague administered the surveys at a pizza party. On rare occasions, forms have been returned with grease or smudges that led us to question the conditions under which they were collected. In one case I was told that faculty suspected a colleague of removing all negative evaluations before taking them to the department office.

Administrative processes must be created and employed that do not permit tainting the results. Smaller errors and omissions in processes, such as failure to encourage honest and thoughtful responses, also result in a loss of confidence in the information collected. Unless sound administrative procedures are followed, dependable information will not be provided.

Abuse 5: Using the Instrument (or the Data Collected) Inappropriately

Occasionally, institutions fail to distinguish, or distinguish inappropriately, among the items on a rating scale. On more than one occasion, individuals made comments similar to the following—"While we have 20 items on our ratings form and allegedly all of them are important in the evaluation process only #7 really matters for making personnel decisions." In other cases, the average of all items may be used to make a judgment about performance without regard to their importance or relevance. An extreme example of this abuse occurred at a campus that found their computer program had included in their summary measure of teaching effectiveness an item about the quality of the rating form. Less extreme abuses occur somewhat frequently as when a global item such as—"Overall I rate this course as excellent"—is given the same importance in a summary measure as less important methods items like—"The instructor encouraged student-faculty interaction outside of class."

Abuse 6: Insufficient Attention to Selecting/Developing an Instrument

The tendency for campuses to rely entirely on student ratings to assess teaching effectiveness is rapidly declining. Campuses that take the evaluation of teaching seriously include student ratings as part of a larger body of evidence (see Chapter 8). The content of the student ratings tool should be determined by both the functions of the rating program and the content of other sources of evaluative information.

How effective teaching is defined is important in identifying the sources of evidence to use and, if student ratings are included, the content of the instrument. While the descriptions of effective teaching in a number of books and articles have consistent themes (Arreola, 2000; Bernstein, 1996; Fink, 2003; Hoyt & Pallett, 1999), important differences are also present. Without a thoughtful discussion of what teaching effectiveness means on your campus (or department), it is unlikely a student ratings tool will be selected or created that will serve your purposes well.

Decisions about the purposes of the instrument will impact the content (Cashin, 1996) and the length of the instrument. If you want to use student ratings to serve purposes beyond personnel evaluation—to guide improvement efforts, offer descriptive information that assists in advising, or serve as a supplemental source of evidence for accreditation—the instrument will need to be longer than one whose only intent is personnel evaluation.

Abuse 7: Failure to Conduct Research to Support the Validity and Reliability of a Student Ratings Tool

When individuals call to inquire about the IDEA student ratings instrument, I usually ask about the student ratings instrument they currently use. Invariably, if it is locally developed, they report having no evidence to support the instrument's validity or reliability. While there are often good reasons to have a locally developed instrument, it is extremely important to establish its credibility through reliability and validity studies. Without such studies, many faculty members (especially those who are psychometrically sophisticated) will lack trust in the instrument. In addition, if a personnel decision is ever challenged in a grievance hearing or lawsuit, those who use the instrument will be on firmer ground if evidence supports the reliability and validity of the system.

Administering Student Ratings Online

Many campuses have either adopted or are considering moving to online administration of student ratings. For distance education, online surveys are clearly the most viable option. But for face-to-face instruction there is less direct control when online surveys are administered outside the classroom than when the ratings process is overseen in class. The many benefits of online administration include more rapid turnaround time, automatic transcribing of comments, and saving class time.

However, there are concerns that need to be addressed. The greatest of these is response rate. When response rates are below 65%, the representativeness of the information collected comes into question. When a high percentage of a class fails to respond to a survey, it is difficult to have confidence that the results obtained would remain the same if nonrespondents had provided feedback. This greatly reduces the value of information collected, at times making it nearly meaningless. The IDEA system response rate when paper forms are used is approximately 80%. When the survey is administered online, it has been in the 45% to 55% range.

But there are exceptions. One campus recently experienced an 86% online response rate. This campus has a long history of viewing student feedback as a valuable resource to guide improvement efforts. Instructors took class time to encourage students to complete the form and periodically reported the percentage of students in the class that had responded. Such a constructive way to attain high response rates seems preferable to plans that penalize nonrespondents by withholding grades for a week or two, although campuses following such policies have reported high response rates.

A less pressing concern expressed about online ratings is group think—the prospect of a number of students completing the form as a group rather than independently. Since students often informally share their views about instructors, the potential for increased impact of this phenomenon may not be great. Nonetheless, it is desirable in the administration process to include instructions about completing the form independently and not consulting with other students.

Losing control of the precise time a survey is administered can be worrisome for faculty. The concern is that when students are allowed two weeks or longer to complete a form that there may be an event (exam, return of a paper) that may have undue influence on how a student responds. Research on this issue may be warranted. However, if results are categorized into only one of a few groups as recommended earlier, the impact of timing should not be great.

As campuses move from paper and pencil to online administration, new questions about the administration process arise. The impact of the loss of administrative control can be examined by reviewing feedback from faculty whose results have been stable over a number of years when using the paper and pencil form. If results are substantially different when online administration is employed, there may be reason for concern.

To obtain acceptable response rates when surveys are administered online, the system needs constant attention. During the administration period, response rates need to be continuously monitored and reported to instructors. They, in turn, should provide this information to their students and emphasize the importance of responding. If a campus has announced a minimally acceptable response rate, the instructors need to know they are responsible to help achieve it.

Conclusion

It is beyond the scope of this chapter to discuss technical issues related to the general reliability and validity of student ratings. While one may find support for nearly any point of view, the preponderance of evidence provides encouragement for the use of student ratings

(Braskamp & Ory, 1994; Cashin, 2003; Centra, 1993; Feldman, 1989; Marsh & Dunkin, 1992). Experience shows that when sound instrument development and administration practices are employed, information obtained is credible.

A good instrument (with proven validity and reliability) does not ensure a sound system for either faculty evaluation or faculty development. Successful implementation requires that the system be understood and endorsed by faculty, administrators, and students and the information be used appropriately and with sensitivity.

Too often student ratings are viewed as the necessary evil. Such attitudes have a negative effect on their benefits. Their value in supporting improvement efforts may actually be enhanced when multiple sources of information are used to evaluate teaching since student ratings are then likely to be deemphasized (appropriately) as part of personnel evaluation. This is especially true when campuses provide resources that permit information obtained from student ratings to facilitate teaching improvement.

If a truly effective student ratings program is developed and appropriately implemented it can contribute positively to teaching improvement and the maintenance of institutional quality.

ACKNOWLEDGMENTS

I would like to thank my IDEA Center colleagues Amy Gross and Donald Hoyt for their helpful comments on earlier drafts of this chapter.

REFERENCES

Arreola, R. A. (2000). *Developing a comprehensive faculty evaluation system: A handbook for college faculty and administrators on designing and operating a comprehensive faculty evaluation system* (2nd ed.). Bolton, MA: Anker.

Bernstein, D. J. (1996, Spring). A departmental system for balancing the development and evaluation of college teaching: A commentary on Cavanagh. *Innovative Higher Education, 20*(4), 241–247.

Braskamp, L. A., & Ory, J. C. (1994). *Assessing faculty work: Enhancing individual and institutional performance.* San Francisco, CA: Jossey-Bass.

Cashin, W. E. (1996, January). *Developing an effective faculty evaluation system* (IDEA Paper No. 33). Manhattan, KS: Center for Faculty Evaluation and Development, Kansas State University.

Cashin, W. E. (2003). Evaluating college and university teaching: Reflections of a practitioner. In J. C. Smart (Ed.), *Higher education: Handbook of theory and research* (Vol. 18, pp. 531–593). Boston, MA: Kluwer.

Centra, J. A. (1993). *Reflective faculty evaluation: Enhancing teaching and determining faculty effectiveness.* San Francisco, CA: Jossey-Bass.

Chickering, A. W., & Gamson, Z. F. (1987, March). Seven principles for good practice in undergraduate education. *AAHE Bulletin, 39*(7), 3–7.

Cohen, P. A. (1980). Effectiveness of student rating feedback for improving college instruction: A meta-analysis of findings. *Research in Higher Education, 13*(4), 321–341.

Davis, B. G. (1993). *Tools for teaching.* San Francisco, CA: Jossey-Bass.

Feldman, K. A. (1989). The association between student ratings of specific instructional dimensions and student achievement: Refining and extending the synthesis of data from multisection validity studies. *Research in Higher Education, 30*(6), 583–645.

Fink, L. D. (2003). *Creating significant learning experiences: An integrated approach to designing college courses.* San Francisco, CA: Jossey-Bass.

Hoyt, D. P., & Pallett, W. H. (1999). *Appraising teaching effectiveness: Beyond student ratings* (IDEA Paper No. 36). Manhattan, KS: The IDEA Center.

Marsh, H. W., & Dunkin, M. (1992). Students' evaluations of university teaching: A multidimensional perspective. In J. C. Smart (Ed.), *Higher education: Handbook of theory and research* (Vol. 8, pp. 143–233). New York, NY: Agathon.

McKeachie, W. J. (2002). *McKeachie's teaching tips: Strategies, research, and theory for college teachers* (11th ed.). Boston, MA: Houghton Mifflin.

Seldin, P. (1999). Current practices—good and bad—nationally. In P. Seldin & Associates, *Changing practices in evaluating teaching: A practical guide to improved faculty performance and promotion/tenure decisions* (pp. 1–24). Bolton, MA: Anker.

Svinicki, M. D. (2004). *Learning and motivation in the postsecondary classroom.* Bolton, MA: Anker.

Zull, J. E. (2002). *The art of changing the brain: Enriching the practice of teaching by exploring the biology of learning.* Sterling, VA: Stylus.

Institutional Service

Clement A. Seldin

5

An assistant professor of political science at a mid-size university in the Midwest was shocked by the recommendations of her department personnel committee. At her three-year mini-tenure review, they urged her to scale down service contributions, especially local community work. She knew her research and publication record was solid and her teaching was excellent. Scale down service? Why? At a meeting with the personnel committee, they applauded her professional portfolio, especially her new research on Jeffersonian democracy. Then they explained the delicate and very important balance of research, teaching, and service at her university. They stated that her personnel materials presented her primary focus as service to the community. They strongly urged that she put much less emphasis on service—until she was tenured.

This story, and others like it, reflect the complexity of what academics believe is the third major component of the professorate: institutional service. While many cite the importance of service contributions for faculty (Arreola, 2000; Boyer, 1990; Williams & Rhodes, 2002), others argue that it is the black sheep of faculty responsibilities because it is poorly defined and rewarded and often unrelated to the primary faculty responsibilities of teaching and research (Berberet, 1999; Crosson, 1985). What is service? Does the college or university want the same level of service as the department? Should professors wait until tenure before engaging in meaningful work in the community? How should service contributions be documented?

To address these and other questions, I reviewed scholarship on the impact of institutional service when faculty are reviewed on annual faculty reports and for promotion, reappointment, and tenure. In addition, I perused many institutional and departmental academic handbooks at different types and sizes of colleges and universities in diverse regions of the United States. I also communicated with academics at several institutions to gain their perspective. These faculty included colleagues I have known for more than 25 years as well as former doctoral students from my own institution who now teach at other universities. In telephone conversations and email communications, I explored many open-ended questions. How is service defined at your institution? How is it valued? How is it defined and considered in your department? What are your experiences at personnel committee meetings when reviewing the service contributions of colleagues? Further, after 27 years at the University of Massachusetts Amherst, I have had considerable experience chairing department and school personnel committees. Over the years, I have engaged in discussion about the value of service in my department, school, and university offices. This background provided the foundation for this chapter.

What Is Institutional Service?

Outreach service includes faculty sharing their expertise as they serve audiences predominately external to the University. This service may include presentations to non-academic professional and learned societies, participation in community affairs as a representative of the University and consulting (whereby the expertise of the faculty is shared for the good of society). Other service based on the expertise of the faculty could include service to government and corporations, advisory boards, policy

analysis, technology transfer, clinical service delivery, and participation in task forces, authorities, and public hearings.

—The Pennsylvania State University (2000)

Service is based upon a faculty member's professional skills and
expertise as they benefit the university, professional organizations, or the community.

—Indiana University–Kokomo (2001)

Faculty should also be . . . "good institutional citizens." The evaluation criterion of public service and contributions to the
growth and development of the college community speaks to
this. Service on college and department committees and task
forces, advising student groups, professionally related community service are some examples of appropriate activity.

—Framingham State College (2004)

In a broad sense, institutional service is using a professor's
knowledge and skills to benefit the institution, professional organizations, and the community. Service has two basic components:
internal (typically on campus) and external (profession and community). Some institutions identify three elements by separating
external service into its two major parts—service to the profession
and service to the community. Regarding *internal service,* the most
commonly cited examples include faculty participation on department and university committees and task forces. However, student
advising, mentoring junior colleagues, serving as teaching observers,
developing workshops and campus functions for colleagues and/or
students to enhance understanding and knowledge, and advising
student groups such as honor societies are also considered internal
service.

External service to the community means participation in various civic groups, agencies, and organizations. Examples include presentations to local groups and organizations; professional advice and

counsel to community groups or individuals; and participation on local cultural, educational, or governmental committees.

External service to the profession means engagement in the broader academic community. Examples of this contribution include serving as editor of a refereed journal; participation as officer of a state, regional, national, or international scholarly society; organizer of a state, regional, national, or international conference; reviewer of conference proposals; editor of conference proceedings; reviewer of proposals for external funding agencies; and consultant to government, business, and industry and membership on their committees.

Regardless of how service is defined, there is a fundamental characteristic that is inherent in the definition: Service means benefit. The skills and expertise of the faculty member should provide unmistakable benefit to individuals, groups, and organizations. Otherwise, it may not be valued by the institution. Boyer (1990) made the argument that one's service contribution must be closely linked to one's professional field. Many institutions make this critical connection explicit in faculty handbooks and on university web sites.

> Although they should not be discouraged from providing service in any field in which they have an interest, it should be understood that faculty activities are, as a general rule, considered to be valid university service only when they are performed using competencies relevant to the faculty member's role and/or area of specialization at the university.
>
> —Washburn University (2005)

The music professor who chairs an ad hoc committee for the public school system that examines orchestral music education in the school district will be applauded for his effort. This is considered bona fide external service. However, if he served on the search committee for a new 11th-grade social studies teacher, the value of this service would be marginal to many institutions. Regardless of the length of service or leadership involvement, unless it is related to the faculty member's discipline and expertise, it may be unrewarded and even discouraged by a college or university. This is a simple reality at many institutions. Moreover, some argue that service must be directly related to the profession or the institution for it to be valued. "The questionable priority and doubtful reward value are especially apparent when the 'service' is public service for individuals and groups external to the campus rather than service to the academic discipline or the institution" (Crosson, 1985, pp. 1–2).

Who Evaluates Institutional Service?

Typically, yearly faculty evaluations are managed by individual departments. These internal department reviews may be shared with the college or university administration but, generally, if the department is supportive, the institution is as well. Of course, at major faculty reviews such as tenure and promotion, there are generally several layers of review, each assessing internal and external service contributions.

Depending on the size and complexity of the institution, a professor can expect a committee or two of his or her peers as well as the department chair and dean to review personnel documents before they are sent to the administration. When it comes to institutional service, one does not know whether the reviewers will be major advocates of internal and external service or individuals who see it as only marginally important. Regardless, it is vital to know the extent to which the university and department values service contributions.

Is Institutional Service Valued by the Institution?

This answer is complex and depends on two factors: 1) the individual institution, and 2) the purpose of faculty review. Virtually all colleges and universities support institutional service, but there is a range of support. In pie-chart terms, the relative size of the three pieces (teaching, research/scholarship, and service) will often depend on the mission of the institution and its classification (research university, doctoral university, master's university, four-year undergraduate college, or community college). Moreover, the type of review (annual faculty report, tenure, promotion, reappointment) may resize the three pie pieces as well.

Some institutions strongly support service activity in personnel decisions and document this commitment in faculty guides. Others may not provide detail of their commitment to service, yet it is understood by faculty that service contributions are far from optional. A former doctoral student at my university who is now an assistant professor at an eastern state university said,

> Service to the school and the greater community is highly valued here. They talk frequently about the importance of "active engagement in the community." Everyone knows it is the real currency at this school and certainly tenure and promotion is more likely with substantial service contributions.

Another veteran state university professor at a different eastern institution explained, "Service here is a given. That means service to the greater community and to the profession. This is loosely explained in our Faculty Guide but everyone knows this is what we stand for."

As noted in the scenario that opened this chapter, some institutions urge faculty to minimize service activities until after tenure and then become actively involved. Arizona State University (1999) encourages junior faculty to focus on research and teaching, asserting that major service contributions are not primary factors for tenure and promotion decisions to associate professor. The University of Washington (2004) takes a similar position. Other institutions place external service (especially community service) a distant third behind teaching and research at all stages of an academic career. Although they may not explicitly record this hierarchy in a faculty handbook, the absence of strong documented support for community service by senior faculty suggests that it is only marginally valued. Stated plainly by a 20-year professor at a prestigious university in the northeast,

> Research and scholarship—that is what gets you tenure and promotion here, not service. Everyone nods and praises your work with local government but it is that multi-million dollar grant and important publication that gets you promoted to full [professor].

The college or university establishes the relative size of the three pie pieces (teaching, research/scholarship, and service). Professors should be well aware of their institution's position and engage in professional work that is consistent with it. While the college or university perspective provides the umbrella under which departments operate, individual departments define and describe valued service contributions for faculty and generally provide more detail.

Is Institutional Service Valued by Departments?

Colleges and universities commonly explain their perspective on institutional service in faculty handbooks. However, it is often a general overview of faculty expectations at key career levels (instructor, lecturer, assistant, associate, and full professor) (see Chapter 7). Departments are left to interpret this broad institutional framework and define service within their discipline. The department must go beyond the institutional structure, document the importance of service, and establish clear performance expectations. This makes for an important value statement based on the perspective of the department, its academic goals, and the mission of the profession. For example, an education department may highly value service by faculty who engage in external activity (lectures, workshops, committee work) with local schools, agencies, or state department of education.

The computer science department may focus more on new, cutting-edge programming on campus but not encourage work with community groups. Because departments emphasize institutional service in different ways, it is especially important that each document how service is defined and its relative value. Importantly, while departments may vary their service expectations, it is vital that departments recognize the culture of the institution in terms of its commitment to service. The worst-case scenario is a professor not following the vision of the institution *or* the department. This is very risky at best, self-defeating at worst.

> My university values research first, teaching second, and service a distant third. In my department, we encourage all pre-tenure faculty to push scholarship and not focus on service. Two years ago, a colleague was up for tenure. Although he had incredible service to schools and education agencies and his teaching was reasonably strong, his research and publications were limited. We had a "paper trail" of annual performance reviews urging him to accelerate his scholarship agenda but he preferred to do "the important work" and didn't really listen. What happened? He didn't get tenure.
>
> —Education professor, large midwestern university

In contrast, a focus on service is generally expected and highly valued at universities that offer many undergraduate programs and have commitment to graduate education through a master's degree (Williams & Rhodes, 2002). Quality teaching is also expected but research and scholarship are not strongly emphasized. At this type of institution, the tenure and promotion review is very different.

> At both the university and department level, comprehensive involvement in community service is the expectation. I served as chair of our department personnel committee last year. We had a very difficult tenure case in which an assistant professor faced

much scrutiny. Why? Because he lacked serious service involvement. He was finally tenured but it was the most difficult case I've seen in 20 years. It took much communication with my provost and her T and P [tenure and promotion] committee. Service to the community and the profession was the key issue.

—Public health professor, southern university
(undergraduate through master's)

At a large state university in the east, the education department valued service to the community and profession more so than did the university, which documented a strong primary focus on research and scholarship. The department urged all faculty, including those untenured, to make a significant difference in the education of students by active involvement in school and community affairs. When personnel cases were reviewed, department committees looked eagerly at service both on campus and at local, state, national, and international levels. The major goal for faculty was to be a catalyst for positive educational change. The university understood this emphasis and tacitly supported it for this specific department. When education professors with outstanding service records and marginal research were considered for tenure and promotion, the university, perhaps reluctantly, generally supported the department's decisions.

Over the last decade, things have changed. A series of top university administrators began to question the department's emphasis on service. Tenure and promotion cases, in which service was highlighted on the positive recommendation, faced more scrutiny. Slowly, over a period of years, there was an evolutionary shift and new education faculty were hired with stronger research and scholarship skills. Expectations began to change, and now, well into the first decade of the 21st century, this education department has shifted its emphasis from service to research. This is a case where the department's value of service gradually changed to become more aligned with the university.

What is the lesson learned from these cases? Should departments follow the lead of the institution? Yes, to some extent. When it comes to institutional service, departments should seriously consider how the college or university values service contributions. It does not mean that a department cannot deviate from the institution's outlook. Certain departments may describe and value service contributions differently than their college or university does. However, departments should be keenly aware of the institutional culture. Not to act in ways consistent with the institution is possible but not advisable.

Is Student Advising Valued as Institutional Service?

Student advising (both academic and social/emotional counseling) is frequently identified as an important aspect of institutional service. Although not highly regarded by some faculty who know they must focus efforts on teaching, research, scholarship, and committee assignments, many institutions expect their faculty to, at a minimum, list their advisees and the latter's academic status (undergraduate or graduate). Doctoral universities may also expect faculty to identify if they chair student committees such as comprehensive or dissertation committees. Implicit in this identification is the belief that chairing doctoral committees is a major commitment and far exceeds student advising in terms of time and intellectual energy.

Employing the listing method addresses the quantity of advising but not the quality. Some institutions urge students to complete advisor evaluations. Short, one-page, anonymous surveys typically use a Likert scale to solicit information on advisor knowledge and availability as well as overall advisor competence. Open-ended questions ask students to comment further on the effectiveness of their advisors (see Appendix E). When the results of these surveys are measured against how the professor describes his or her advising, a faculty review committee may gain a unique perspective from which to assess faculty advising.

Our undergraduate and graduate students complete Advisor Evaluation forms every year. Our faculty also write their overall philosophy about student advising. It is fascinating to compare the two. In most cases, there is high level consistency. Occasionally (like one last year), there is amazing inconsistency almost to the point of humor. As chair of the department, I read this and, although advising is not a major part of our evaluation system, it did affect my written comments as chair on those reviews.

—Chair and professor, College of Social Sciences,
midwestern university

How Should Institutional Service Be Documented?

It is essential to know how the institution and individual departments describe and value service, but it is also important to know how best to document service activities. Some faculty simply list service contributions with dates and brief descriptions. But this is not a case of less is more. Carefully and fully documenting service contributions provides greater understanding and value of this work (see Chapter 13).

At major reviews such as tenure or promotion, some universities specifically request that service contributions be documented in a particular way. For example, Emory University (1999) requests that "[Tenure materials] should include a statement that defines service and describes how the service of the candidate was evaluated. The description of service should include service both to Emory and to the world beyond." Kansas State University (2005) requests a two-page summary of service contributions with evidence of leadership.

Implicit at these and many other institutions is the need to document the benefit to the college or university and the external community. A simple laundry list of committees, presentations, and workshops is insufficient. How can a personnel committee accurately assess one's service without knowing more about the activities? Although a simple listing addresses the issue of quantity, it is not enough to document the quality. Consider the following example. Professor A has served on three department committees and two university committees. An initial assessment might suggest that she has provided greater service than Professor B, who has served on only one department committee and one university committee. The work of personnel committees is often so demanding that unless detail shows the dimensions of each committee involvement, a personnel committee may conclude that Professor A has provided greater benefit. Of course, this assumption may be flawed. A closer look may reveal that both committees on which Professor B served met weekly and each member had major responsibilities. Professor B may have assumed a leadership role in preparing reports (even though she was not chair). Unless this is carefully documented, a personnel committee review may be inaccurate at best and unfair at worst.

Some may argue that an inaccurate understanding of service contributions will make no difference in the ultimate decision to tenure, promote, or reappoint. However, even at research universities, where service contributions are generally less important than research/scholarship and teaching, on rare occasions institutional service may be a significant factor. A senior professor who has taught at several major research institutions and chaired many personnel committees pointed out that

> Institutional service is always acknowledged but, in my experience over a 30-year career, it is research and scholarship that is number one—followed by teaching. Service comes in a distant third. Please note, however, I have seen a few cases over the years where important and meaningful institutional service tipped the balance on a tenure or promotion decision.

Professors who are the most successful in promoting the richness of their institutional service go well beyond simply listing contributions and providing some detail. Rather, they document their service, briefly describe it and their role, and provide evidence of benefit. In this way, personnel committees can better understand the nature and importance of the service. For example, which information looks stronger in an annual faculty report, A or B?

A) Membership on University Computer Committee, 2005–2006.

B) Membership on University Computer Committee, 2005–2006. This six-member team (one faculty member from each college) met weekly to redesign the computer access system for all students. I chaired the budget subcommittee and served as senior author on the budget report. Based on our recommendations, the university has funded a pilot effort for fall 2007. It will provide greater student access to campus computers, more efficient troubleshooting and computer repair at less student expense. Attached is my subcommittee report and a letter of appreciation from the committee chair, Professor W. Kellogg.

Certainly option B provides more complete and impressive documentation and includes evidence of benefit to the university.

A simple listing of committee membership, related association participation, and conference involvement does not provide sufficient detail for a personnel committee to gain a genuine understanding of the scope and benefit of particular contributions. While few will eagerly read lengthy discussion of each committee, presentation, or consultation, a brief description including faculty role and its benefit to the institution, department, or profession is extremely useful. In addition, written products of this service such as letters or certificates of appreciation can provide direct evidence of the level of faculty engagement and the benefit to the institution, department, or profession.

Conclusion

Institutional service is important. College and university faculty are experts in their fields and have an array of skills that can provide substantial benefit to a department, institution, profession, and the greater community. However, expectations for service depend, to a large extent, on the type of institution, specific academic department, and the purpose of the personnel review. Although many argue that institutional service is generally the smallest piece of the pie, it merits more complete and accurate documentation.

REFERENCES

Arizona State University. (1999, May 6). *Criteria for tenure and promotion.* Retrieved December 22, 2005, from the Arizona State University, College of Education web site: http://coe.asu.edu/personnel/criteriafinal99.html

Arreola, R. A. (2000). *Developing a comprehensive faculty evaluation system: A handbook for college faculty and administrators on designing and operating a comprehensive faculty evaluation system* (2nd ed.). Bolton, MA: Anker.

Berberet, J. (1999, September). The professoriate and institutional citizenship: Toward a scholarship of service. *Liberal Education, 85*(4), 33–39.

Boyer, E. L. (1990). *Scholarship reconsidered: Priorities of the professoriate.* Princeton, NJ: Carnegie Foundation for the Advancement of Teaching.

Crosson, P. H. (1985). *Public service in higher education: Practices and priorities.* Washington, DC: Association for the Study of Higher Education, ERIC Clearinghouse on Higher Education. (ERIC Document Reproduction Service No. ED284515). Retrieved December 22, 2005, from http://www.eric.ed.gov/ERICDocs/data/ericdocs2/content_storage_01/0000000b/80/2a/0b/4e.pdf

Emory University. (1999, February 18). *Tenure and promotion: University guidelines for candidate files.* Retrieved December 22, 2005, from the Emory University, Office of the Provost web site: http://www.emory.edu/PROVOST/tenurepromotion_files/tenure.htm

Framingham State College. (2004). *2004–2005 faculty resource guide.* Retrieved January 20, 2006, from the Framingham State College, Office of Academic Affairs web site: http://www.framingham.edu/AcademicAffairs/resource_guide/faculty_policies.htm

Indiana University Kokomo. (2001, October 22). *IUK promotion and tenure criteria.* Retrieved January 20, 2006, from the Indiana University Kokomo, Office of Academic Affairs web site: http://www.iuk.edu/~koacad/handbook/tenure.htm

Kansas State University. (2005, August 16). *Guidelines for the organization and format of tenure and promotion documentation.* Retrieved December 22, 2005, from the Kansas State University, Office of Academic Services web site: http://www.ksu.edu/academicservices/forms/promotio.html

The Pennsylvania State University. (2000, February 1). *Senate agenda.* Retrieved December 22, 2005, from The Pennsylvania State University, University Faculty Senate web site: http://www.senate.psu.edu/agenda/feb01-00agn/feb01-00agn.html

University of Washington. (2004, Fall). *Promotion and tenure guidelines.* Retrieved December 22, 2005, from the University of Washington, College of Arts and Sciences web site: http://www.artsci.washington.edu/Services/Personnel/Promten guide.htm

Washburn University. (2005). *The core of academe: Teaching, scholarly activity, and service.* Retrieved December 22, 2005, from the Washburn University web site: http://www.washburn.edu/admin/fac-handbook/FHAPP2.htm

Williams, K. F., & Rhodes, T. M. (2002, April). *Chief academic officers' perceptions about faculty evaluation.* Paper presented at the 83rd annual meeting of the American Educational Research Association, New Orleans, LA.

Peer Observations as a Catalyst for Faculty Development

6

Barbara J. Millis

Nearly 15 years ago, when I received a Fund for the Improvement of Postsecondary Education grant to strengthen a peer visit program at the University of Maryland University College, I discovered that institutions with open classroom doors were a rarity. I was invited to do a few workshops—but only a few—including one at a major research institution where the provost cheerfully introduced me to a roomful of chairs and then exited, leaving me feeling like Daniel in the lion's den. I quietly put away my prepared presentation and gulped, "Let's talk about classroom observations. What do you currently do?" In fact, at that point I couldn't give away a workshop for chairs—or anyone—on classroom observations. The prevailing mood was much like the "Welcome to the Academy" cartoon by Signe Wilkerson with intense faculty members on individual islands in shark-infested waters. They hold aloft signs saying, "Bug Off," "Keep Out," and "No Trespassing." This personal observation was confirmed by an article written by a scholar from the UK who described the 1980s in the U.S. as a time when the peer review of teaching was "dormant" (D'Andrea, 2002).

The Current Climate for Peer Review of Teaching

Happily, that climate has changed, thanks in large part to groundbreaking work by Lee Shulman, Patricia Hutchings, Peter Seldin, and Nancy Chism. Much of the credit goes to the former American

Association for Higher Education (AAHE), which launched the two-year project "From Idea to Prototype: The Peer Review of Teaching" in January 1994. Since then, classroom observations have become much more business as usual, often for a wide range of purposes such as promotion and tenure requirements, department accountability, teaching awards, intrinsically motivated desires to excel, and collegiality. At present, classroom observations are often discussed within the context of the peer review of teaching, which includes broader components such as "teaching circles, mentoring, classroom visits, course portfolios, the pedagogical colloquium, and a few others, all of which are documented and reported on in *Making Teaching Community Property*, . . . published by AAHE in 1996" (Pat Hutchings, personal communication, June 14, 2005). The current Peer Review of Teaching Project, funded by the Pew Charitable Trusts and the Hewlitt Foundation, is described by Hutchings as a "consortium of six research institutions [that] develop campus communities that explore and apply peer review for documenting, promoting, and valuing the intellectual work of teaching." Peer classroom observations have been increasingly linked, as well, to the scholarship of teaching and learning (D'Andrea, 2002). In fact, Hutchings concludes,

> Classroom observation might well be adapted to the purposes of the scholarship of teaching and learning. The key point, perhaps, is that the scholarship of teaching is not an evaluation of classroom practice (and of course sometimes classroom observation *does* serve this function) but an inquiry, an investigation, into some question that the teacher sees as important to practice in his or her classroom or field. When classroom observation serves inquiry, it can certainly be a tool for the scholarship of teaching and learning.

As Hutchings suggests, the literature on classroom observations often addresses the prickly issue of observations intended for summative evaluation (often linked to promotion and tenure) and formative evaluation (often linked to faculty development). Although the final use of the data collected may vary, the *process* of collecting the data—the classroom observation itself—should remain the same, a point made in 1989 (Millis) and earlier, if based only on the economics of supporting two different faculty assessment practices. Svinicki and Lewis (n.d.) similarly find the two purposes mutually supportive:

> Although the outcomes of formative and summative observation are different, effective formative peer observation serves as a vehicle for effective summative peer observation and evaluation at the departmental level. Most authors believe that the two processes are compatible and mutually supportive of faculty involvement in either formative or summative peer observation. (p. 5)

The Basics of Classroom Observations and Review of Course Materials

The basics of classroom observations have been spelled out repeatedly (Arreola, 2000; Brinko & Menges, 1997; Chism, 1999; Keig & Waggoner, 1994; Lewis & Lunde, 2001; Millis, 1992). Regardless of their purpose, it is critically important to follow a three-step process for observations: a *previsit consultation,* where the visitor and the faculty member discuss a range of topics, either face-to-face or via phone or email, and the visitor reviews the syllabus and other relevant class materials; the *visit itself;* and the critically important *follow-up visit,* where the two parties exchange ideas and observations.

For the *previsit consultation,* I like to start with the context of the class. What are the overall course objectives? What are the objectives for the particular class I will observe? How do you expect to achieve these objectives or goals? Where does this course fit in the curriculum? Who are the students? What have you asked them to do in preparation for this class? Is this class typical of your teaching or are you introducing new approaches, techniques, or methodologies? Are there any problem areas, such as cliques or dominating students, that I should watch out for? What has preceded the lesson?

Then I move to the faculty member's expectations of me. What should I read or review prior to the visit? What two or three things do you want me to focus on for this observation? (I suggest topics such as pacing, clarity, and so on.) What do you hope to achieve from my visit(s)? (The answer to this question often depends on the purpose of the visit.) What final product do you expect me to provide? (For example, oral feedback, a formal report, or a written summary that can go into a teaching portfolio.)

I review the syllabus and any relevant course materials within the context of this pre-observation discussion and preparation. The syllabus, for instance, should spell out the overall course objectives and the context for the particular class. I also read it carefully to determine if objectives, assessment, and activities are aligned. If, for example, a stated objective in a given course is to challenge students to think critically and to solve problems using higher-level thinking skills, then I look carefully at the assignments and examinations. The examinations, in particular, should reflect the objectives: multiple-choice and true/false exams are not likely to encourage or reinforce higher-level thinking skills. Three useful sources for checklists and peer review forms for course materials appear in Braskamp and Ory (1994), Chism (1999), and Weimer, Parrett, and Kerns (2002).

We then discuss the logistics for the visit. Where will the visitor sit? (I recommend about three-quarters of the way from the front of the room next to as many students as possible, not at the back or on the periphery.) Should the visitor be introduced? (Absolutely.) What role will the visitor play during the visit? (It's up to the instructor. I have served as a peer editor along with composition teachers, been a fly on the wall, or contributed to in-class discussions. Some disconcerting roles can occur when the observer is expected to be the expert. I remember my adrenalin pumping when a composition teacher unexpectedly said, "That's a very arcane grammar point: Let's ask our distinguished visitor." More benignly, in an ESL classroom, I was asked to give a native speaker's pronunciation of key words.) How will the feedback be offered? (This decision is usually determined by the purpose of the visit. I often provide oral feedback before writing a more formal report, particularly if I am preparing a single summary report based on multiple visits.)

The *visit itself* should unfold as the two parties have discussed. The teacher introduces the visitor, who is sitting three-quarters of the way into the classroom and participating as the two agreed. But be open to unexpected opportunities. For example, when a University of Nevada–Reno professor decided to have his class simulate a battle between the Redcoats and the Colonials, I made a snap decision to join one of the lines, dropping to my knees to "reload" as the students in the row behind pretended to "fire." This worthwhile experience reinforced for me the power of active learning.

The *follow-up visit* (sometimes called a debriefing) should provide reflective insights into what the observer saw, what the teacher intended, and what the probable outcomes—particularly the impact on student learning—might be. To give the teacher ownership of the feedback, I try to start with probing questions. How do you think things went? What was the best thing about today's lesson? What would you change? What do you think students learned? When I offer feedback, I try to emphasize choices around what I have observed—"Your Venn diagram could not be seen at the back of the room. Could you consider a larger sketch, a handout for students, or a PowerPoint projection?" I describe things as concretely as possible—"The student responses I observed suggested positive rapport: They clustered around you before class, joking and asking questions; 85% participated during the discussion on vehicular suicide; 18 apples were carefully aligned on your desk." I also focus, using action verbs, on future changes. Overall, the goal of a feedback session should be twofold: to reinforce the teacher's good practices, providing reinforcement and confidence, and to offer the motivation and knowledge for positive changes to strengthen teaching.

Just as this post-conference discussion helps both parties to reflect on effective teaching practices, the observation process bene-fits both parties. The visitors, even experienced ones who might be considered mentors, can gain a great deal from observations and subsequent reflection, which can in turn influence teaching innova-tions, insights into campus life, and content knowledge.

Building Departmental Buy-In for Classroom Observations

Given the benefits both parties accrue, classroom observations can be a powerful force for department cohesion. If departments emphasize formative evaluation, voluntary faculty involvement in evaluation can positively affect department "morale and collegial climate" (Keig & Waggoner, 1994, p. 128). However, individual faculty members may remain opposed to observations unless there is a concerted depart-ment push to make them relevant, developmental, collegial, and fair. Massy, Wilger, and Colbeck (1994) list peer evaluation as one of sev-eral factors in departments that support effective teaching. McNinch (n.d) notes that "if colleagues, in assessing the teaching of their peers, can agree on the appropriateness of the data gathering observation process and instruments, they will have taken an important first step in assessing and improving teaching in higher education." Often a good starting point for discussion is the observation instrument itself. If there is agreement on the instrument, then the visits are more like-ly to occur according to mutually agreed-upon guidelines. Getting departmental buy-in for a well-designed observation instrument takes careful planning and cooperation. I recommend a focused nar-rative for the instrument, one that reflects well-thought-out teaching criteria but that allows the observer to take notes holistically. I typi-cally jot down notes as a student would, providing a rich context, but in the margins of my legal tablet I make notes as an observer (e.g., "Students seem confused here. Many were frowning, whispering to neighbors, and thumbing through their textbooks.").

Three Department Models for Designing or Redesigning an Observation Instrument

A Traditional Model

I met with the graduate program director of the University of Nevada–Reno's atmospheric sciences program to discuss how this interdisciplinary unit might initiate a classroom observation process. After conducting an interactive workshop that covered the nuts and bolts of professional classroom visits, the participants were convinced of the benefits of peer classroom observations and formed a subcommittee to review a thick packet of observation instruments I had given them. They next prepared a "straw man" instrument they felt would fit faculty needs and sent it for review to other faculty members, who provided constructive feedback. This process allows all faculty to be involved in the final product but with a minimum of individual effort. This type of committee-based involvement in the development of an evaluative instrument is fairly common in academic departments.

A Participatory Model

Jim Greenberg, from the Center for Faculty Excellence at the University of Maryland, created a participatory activity that I have often encouraged faculty to adopt for departmental development of instruments. It begins with a broad focus. A chair or other facilitator asks faculty members, working individually, to fill in a table with the heading "My Evaluation of Teaching" and two columns: "What I Would Evaluate" and "How I Would Do It." After faculty have worked for five minutes or more, the facilitator asks them to draw a line and start a new table labeled "A Supervisor Evaluating Me," with two similar columns: "What I Would Want Evaluated" and "How I Would Want the Supervisor to Assess It." Participants conduct paired discussions, noting similarities and differences in their responses. Then the debriefing begins. Using a flipchart or overhead transparency the facilitator presents a series of responses divided into two columns: "What Should Be Evaluated" on the left and "How It Can Be Evaluated" on the right. In the right column all references to classroom observations are highlighted (see Figure 6.1 for sample entries).

Figure 6.1   Sample Evaluation Responses

What Should Be Evaluated	How It Can Be Evaluated
Rapport with students	Student interviews
	Classroom observations
	Student evaluations
Subject matter knowledge	Review of course materials
	Review of publications
	Classroom observations
	Informal discussions

This activity serves several purposes. For one, classroom observations are often cited as a valid way of measuring faculty performance, a fact that reinforces the need for departmental use of them. But it is important to note that the right column also captures the departmental view of what should be measured. This list helps to identify the criteria for good teaching. In fact, these entries could be categories on the department's observation instrument.

I always conclude this activity by presenting a summary of Feldman's (1988) groundbreaking article, "Effective College Teaching from the Students' and Faculty's View: Matched or Mis-Matched Priorities?" We compare the nine criteria for good teaching from

Feldman's research—knowledge of the subject/discipline, course preparation and organization, clarity and understandability, enthusiasm for subject/teaching, sensitivity to and concern with students' level and learning progress, availability and helpfulness, quality of examinations, impartiality in evaluating students, overall fairness to students— with the criteria generated by the faculty members. This comparison leads to further discussion of an observation instrument that reflects well-thought-out components of good teaching.

An Innovative Model

A colleague and I developed a series of structured activities that allowed supervisors observing student teachers to redesign the classroom observation instrument. The same model would be highly effective for a disciplinary department either designing or redesigning an instrument. The activity is modeled on a cooperative learning team rotation activity called Send-a-Problem (Millis & Cottell, 1998). Teams of faculty worked on one specific teaching component (Team One initially worked on Component One, Team Two on Component Two, etc). After approximately 40 minutes, each team rotated to another component (one number higher), where they worked without knowing what the previous team had contributed. During a third rotation, each team worked on a third component. During the fourth and final rotation, each team reviewed the input from the three other teams and prepared a synthesis that combined the best ideas and clearest phrasing from all of the groups.

This process began when the participants arrived for a half-day retreat. As they signed in, they drew a playing card that randomly determined their assignment to a four-person team. The current observation instrument focused on five broad components of good teaching (called domains): knowing your students, planning for instruction, delivery and management of instruction, assessment, and professionalism. We arranged five easels, one for each domain, around the meeting area (a large private home), with four large posters containing instructions attached to each easel.

The first three posters, in blue, were identical. They specified two tasks: "Task A: Brainstorm five to eight phrases that best describe this domain and write them below. The phrases must be observable and measurable"; "Task B: List three to five key questions for this domain. These questions should capture what you think needs to be addressed in the observer's comments." A third task, the equivalent of a "sponge" or "extension" activity in cooperative learning, was optional. It challenged participants to prepare a feedback session with these instructions: "You are planning a feedback session based on your observation of this domain. List the concrete suggestions you would make to generate productive change and desired outcomes."

To be certain that no ideas would be lost, we also instructed the participants to write down any phrases, questions, or suggestions that fit another domain. These were left at a designated spot for later use during the synthesis.

The fourth and final poster we attached to each easel was in yellow and contained instructions for designing a synthesis based on input from all four teams working on the given domain. It is important to note that easels and large posters are not essential. Most academics might be more comfortable with the traditional Send-a-Problem format of preprinted worksheets that each team places in a file folder after completion (see Appendix 6.1).

Each four-member group met at the designated easel. The discussions within each group included issues directly related to the given task such as the need to clarify or eliminate ambiguous terms in the current instrument; the desirability of combining overlapping categories; the need to align all assessment measures; the challenge of writing criteria that are both observable and measurable; the need for concise phrasing through active verbs and precise, not wordy, language. From a faculty development standpoint, however, these discussions generated a collegial sharing of best practices in both teaching and in serving as an observer.

Classroom observations, regardless of how they are eventually used, can play a crucial role in faculty development. The most obvious person to benefit is the individual observed, but the observer, too, often learns from the experiences. To provide the greatest impact, an entire department should be invested in the observation process, including development of the instrument and the guidelines for review. Svinicki and Lewis (n.d.) offer 13 concrete suggestions for departments wanting to include peer observation as a part of peer evaluation, including training the visitors and developing and redesigning observation forms. The payoffs can be enormous. As Weimer (1990) notes, "[Observations] need to be an ongoing part of teaching. They keep instructors fresh, encourage and develop accurate self-assessment, and make obvious the complexities of the teaching-learning phenomenon" (p. 122).

REFERENCES

Arreola, R. A. (2000). *Developing a comprehensive faculty evaluation system: A handbook for college faculty and administrators on designing and operating a comprehensive faculty evaluation system* (2nd ed.). Bolton, MA: Anker.

Braskamp, L. A., & Ory, J. C. (1994). *Assessing faculty work: Enhancing individual and institutional performance.* San Francisco, CA: Jossey-Bass.

Brinko, K. T., & Menges, R. J. (Eds.). (1997). *Practically speaking: A sourcebook for instructional consultants in higher education.* Stillwater, OK: New Forums Press.

Chism, N. V. N. (1999). *Peer review of teaching: A sourcebook.* Bolton, MA: Anker.

D'Andrea, V. (2002). *Peer review of teaching in the USA.* Retrieved January 26, 2006, from http://www.heacademy.ac.uk/resources.asp?process=full_record&section=generic&id=29

Feldman, K. A. (1988). Effective college teaching from the students' and faculty's view: Matched or mis-matched priorities? *Research in Higher Education, 28*(4), 291–344.

Hutchings, P. (1996). *Making teaching community property: A menu for peer collaboration and peer review.* Washington, DC: American Association for Higher Education.

Keig, L., & Waggoner, M. D. (1994). *Collaborative peer review: The role of faculty in improving college teaching* (ASHE-ERIC Higher Education Report No. 2). Washington, DC: School of Education and Human Development, The George Washington University.

Lewis, K. G., & Lunde, J. T. P. (Eds.). (2001). *Face to face: A sourcebook of individual consultation techniques for faculty/instructional developers.* Stillwater, OK: New Forums Press.

Massy, W. F., Wilger, A. K., & Colbeck, C. (1994, July/August). Overcoming "hollowed" collegiality. *Change, 26*(4), 10–20.

McNinch, J. (n.d.). *Peer reviews of teaching.* Retrieved December 22, 2005, from the University of Regina, Teaching Development Centre web site: http://www.uregina.ca/tdc/PEEREVALUATION.htm

Millis, B. J. (1989). Colleagues helping colleagues: A peer observation program model. *Journal of Staff, Program, and Organizational Development, 7*(1), 15–21.

Millis, B. J. (1992). Conducting effective peer classroom observations. In D. H. Wulff & J. D. Nyquist (Eds.), *To improve the academy: Vol. 11. Resources for faculty, instructional, and organizational development* (pp. 189–206). Stillwater, OK: New Forums Press.

Millis, B. J., & Cottell, P. J., Jr. (1998). *Cooperative learning for higher education faculty*. Phoenix, AZ: ACE/Oryx Press.

Svinicki, M., & Lewis, K. (n.d.) *Preparing for peer observation: A guidebook*. Retrieved December 22, 2005, from the University of Texas at Austin, Center for Teaching Effectiveness web site: http://www.utexas.edu/academic/cte/PeerObserve.html

University of Nebraska–Lincoln. (n.d.). *Peer review of teaching project: Making visible the intellectual work of teaching*. Retrieved December 23, 2005, from the University of Nebraska–Lincoln, Peer Review of Teaching Project web site: http://www.unl.edu/peerrev/about.html

Weimer, M. (1990). *Improving college teaching: Strategies for developing instructional effectiveness*. San Francisco, CA: Jossey-Bass.

Weimer, M., Parrett, J. L., &. Kerns, M-M. (2002). *How am I teaching? Forms and activities for acquiring instructional input*. Madison, WI: Atwood.

Appendix 6.1
Sample Worksheet

If you come up with phrases, questions, or suggestions that fit another of the five teaching components, write them on the index cards at this station and then put them in the folder for that specific component.

Teaching Component One

Task A: Brainstorm five to eight phrases that best describe this teaching component and write them below. The phrases must be observable and measurable.

1. _____   5. _____

2. _____   6. _____

3. _____   7. _____

4. _____   8. _____

Task B: List three to five key questions for this component. These questions should capture what you think needs to be addressed in the observer's comments.

1. _____   4. _____

2. _____   5. _____

3. _____

Task C: Optional: You are planning a feedback session based on your observation of this teaching component. List the concrete suggestions you would make to generate productive change and desired outcomes.

Self-Evaluation: Composing an Academic Life Narrative

7

Thomas V. McGovern

Our reflections about academic life begin as early as the essay submitted for admission to an undergraduate college. By the end of graduate studies, we have learned the art of constructing a curriculum vitae to list our accomplishments in teaching, scholarship, and service. Almost every year thereafter, individuals in evaluative positions ask us to submit a record of activities to merit consideration for some reward by the academy. All of these moments require the production of a structured text in the interest of fostering fair comparisons about levels of excellence across many individuals. Seldin (2004) documented how the use of portfolios broadened the types of evidence deemed worthy of consideration for these comparisons. Korn (2002) described how portfolios are important after tenure decisions when their construction is no longer just for survival, but for continuing reflection and renewal. Both authors recommended personally constructed narratives to articulate the why and how, and not just the what, of an academic record.

The theme of this chapter is that a capacity for reflection and self-evaluation—from undergraduate college studies to retirement planning—is a critical ingredient in a professor's life. Academic appointments, promotions, honors and recognitions, even annual salary increase reviews, are intermittent reinforcements in a career, but they are, almost always, highly scripted processes for judgments made by others. In contrast, there is the significant internal satisfaction that comes with periodic appraisals of an increasing sophistication in how we think, write, and communicate our ideas to diverse audiences.

Using a developmental framework, I will describe a narrative method that structures faculty members' reflections about self-determined renewal over the course of an academic career.

Identity and Academic Life Development

Erikson and Erikson's (1997) topography of psychosocial, epigenetic conflicts is an apt map for faculty members' development. The conflict of *identity versus identity confusion* defines the tasks required during the second decade of life, often simultaneous with high school education and undergraduate study. Identity is a synthesis of ideals, aspirations, occupational interests, abilities, ideologies, and values. During adolescence and early adulthood, we encounter significant teachers and role models as well as peer group members who support or negate early articulations of who we are and who we hope to become. It was the Eriksons' wise interpretation that we resolve in new ways many of these same conflicts at every subsequent stage. The next conflict of *intimacy versus isolation* addresses personal relationships. Although intimacy often focuses on the exploration of individuals' sexualities, the affiliated dimensions of teaching and learning, mentoring, and collegiality are also established in graduate school and during the years of our first academic appointments. Balancing the motivations of competition and collaboration is an important professional task during the early stages of a career. *Generativity versus stagnation* concerns become more salient during professors' middle stages as the virtue of care and the tasks of teaching teachers and mentoring junior colleagues emerge. The Eriksons' *integrity versus despair* stage captures the affirming recognitions at the zenith of an academic career as well as the sobering reflections when the certainties of achievements may recede. We must genuinely consider the strengths and limitations of our legacies as we prepare for the fruitful potentials of post-retirement.

The three principal activities of academic life—teaching, scholarship, and service—can be integrated into these developmental

themes of identity, intimacy, generativity, and ego integrity. As undergraduates, we observe and seek out good teachers, try our hands at
scholarly writing to advance in a disciplinary or professional field, and
begin a pattern of contributions to campus or community groups. In
graduate school, time devoted to the three activities varies; the ends or
products may shift with opportunities and increasing expertise. Over
the traditional transitions from first appointment as assistant professor to promotion to associate professor with tenure, and to full professor, the energy expended and value ascribed to each of the three activities may vary considerably. Finding the right balance that addresses
our internal psychological needs while recognizing the power of external, institutional environments to prescribe their mix is one of the
continuing judgments to be made and thoroughly consistent with the
Eriksons' developmental framework.

Specific Conflicts of Academic Life

When faculty members address broader developmental themes and
recalibrate the balances among the three principal activities of teaching, scholarship, and service, their choices revolve around specific
conflicts. Figure 7.1 integrates the broader themes with the principal
activities and specific conflicts.

Teaching: Choosing a Type of Institutional Mission and Working With Types of Students

American higher education created multiple types of institutional
settings with differentiated missions. They serve an array of student
populations with diverse characteristics of age, socioeconomic experience, ethnic heritage, prior learning experiences, and registration
patterns. Since the first academic course of study at Harvard
University in the 17th century, institutions offered curricula that fos-
tered both liberal arts learning and career or specialized knowledge
and skills development. Although every type of institution may tout

Figure 7.1 Schema Integrating Broader Developmental Themes With Specific Conflicts

Eriksons' Epigenetic Themes Over the Lifespan
Identity > Intimacy > Generativity > Ego integrity

Principal Activities of Academic Life
Teaching + Scholarship + Service

Specific Conflicts of Academic Life Organized by Activity
Teaching
- Types of institutional missions
- Types of students

Scholarship
- Disciplinary versus interdisciplinary
- Paradigm versus narrative orientation

Service
- Faculty versus administrative roles
- On- versus off-campus contributions

Synthesis
- Public versus private life

the scholar-teacher as the ideal faculty member, teaching assignments and scholarly productivity expectations vary considerably. Thus, from the very first choice that we made for our baccalaureate degree, we were exposed to models of the professoriate by virtue of the type of institution where we studied. Seeking a first position after graduate school, we chose to emulate those early models or to shift to a different type of mission and student body and its concomitant proportions of time available to balance teaching and scholarly excellence. As we progress through the traditional academic ranks, we must also consider how the type of institution and students affect our teaching commitments and define the parameters of available time we devote to our scholarship and service activities.

Scholarship: Disciplinary Versus Interdisciplinary and Paradigm Versus Narrative Orientation

Lower-division general education or core curricula exposed us to the breadth of intellectual subject matter in the arts and humanities, social sciences, sciences, and introductory professional courses. One of the critical, early choices we make is about a subject matter to pursue in more depth. A major field or professional area becomes attractive by virtue of compelling ideas delivered by inspiring scholar-practitioners and the discovery of our own talents in that particular field. As undergraduates, graduate students, and especially as newly appointed assistant professors, we confront a plethora of content and methods for the scholarly creation and communication of knowledge. Some commit to a single discourse community. Others are adroit at navigating the interstices or boundaries. Choosing a dissertation topic and developing a fledgling scholarly program are related to how we resolve conflicts in disciplinary versus interdisciplinary subject matters. Our continuing research programs advance methodologies that build paradigms as opposed to creating narratives.

Service: Faculty Versus Administrative Roles and On- Versus Off-Campus Contributions

Bellah, Madsen, Sullivan, Swidler, and Tipton (1985) interpreted "getting involved" and "being a citizen" as classic and expected virtues in American culture. Academic life places a similar value on faculty governance for deciding on curricular and personnel standards and participative decision-making roles for the development of the institution. After establishing the quality of our scholarship and teaching, we receive invitations to participate on editorial review boards and governance committees for learned societies and professional associations at local, regional, national, or global levels. At some institutions, becoming the department chair is a matter of chronological inevitability, with possible promotions to higher administrative positions beyond the department.

Beginning with our patterns of involvement as undergraduates in service organizations and participation on committees or task forces in graduate school, we implicitly address the demands for investing our intellectual and interpersonal talents in service roles. In many institutions, assistant professors are protected from service responsibilities so that they can build a sturdy platform of teaching and scholarly performance. With promotion to associate professor, and especially with tenure and increasing seniority, there is the explicit call for more service and the assumption of more leadership roles. The conflicts of a faculty versus administrative identity become salient in advanced ranks because we must reduce our teaching activities and continuing scholarly efforts in order to build programs, campuses, or professional organizations, and we necessarily must spend more time off our campuses than on them.

Public Versus Private Life

The dimension of public versus private life intersects with all our decisions about how we spend our time on teaching, scholarship, and service activities. Personal relationships and family commitments constantly slide up and down our priority lists. Long hours in the lab or library, research or leadership positions in distant places and for extended periods stress the individual psyche and our relationships. As we age, our physical and emotional well-being may be factored into decisions about how we spend our time. We always knew that there were 168 hours in every week. If we assume that the typical academic sleeps about 42 hours a week, then how do we spend our 126 waking hours?

After a severe medical problem I encountered at age 50, having been a department chair for 10 years, I was out of work for one year,

and forced to review my hours and my chosen mix of the three traditional academic activities. My calculus for effective time management shifted as part of a revised academic narrative. I discovered that
there were 525,600 minutes in a year that deserved to be savored and
the commitment of time for teaching, scholarship, and service needed to be balanced with more private versus public time.

Life Story Model of Academic Identity

McAdams (1996) found that as we collect life's episodes, we integrate
the "different autobiographical accounts into a narrated whole, aiming
to construct a Me that exhibits a modicum of unity, coherence, and
purpose" (pp. 306–307). Blending Erikson, narrative psychology theory, and literary theory, he developed a life story model of identity.
There are multiple stories within all of us. With a creative metaphor,
McAdams (2001) affirmed his belief in the person's discovery of a unified identity in this way: "People carry with them and bring into conversation a wide range of self-stories, and these stories are nested in
larger and overlapping stories, creating ultimately a kind of *anthology
of the self*" (italics added, p. 117). McAdams and Logan (2004) further
described the critical importance, during the generativity phase, for
individuals to extract new meanings from their remembered episodes
and to work on revisions of their anthologies.

As with Korn's (2002) teaching portfolios for the post-tenure
period, I recommend that faculty compose holistic narratives to
complement the scripted formats of the curriculum vitae or probationary review dossier. To get through any given year, faculty may
have to focus their attention on specific conflict dimensions, but it is
in the storied anthology of the self that we may discover a deeper
sense of identity as professors. In the following pages, I list prompt-
ing questions as starting points to compose a narrative.

Reflection Prompts for an Academic Life Narrative

A life span perspective offers the framework to see choices as part of a connected process, one less scripted by the constraints and demands of the social environments in which we all work. Earlier choices, unarticulated in undergraduate and graduate school contexts, may be remembered with newly significant meanings as one's academic story changes over time. Different institutions and different disciplines have different trajectories for an academic career, so my brackets for the questions are necessarily broad. Similar to Erikson's stage theory, however, the prompts remain important despite how "off-time" they may be in individual cases. All of the prompts were written in the past tense for a uniform style. Readers, beginning with graduate students, can reframe them to facilitate individual reflection, group discussions, or goal-setting purposes. The sequence of questions within each bracket follows the order of the principal activities—teaching, scholarship, service—and, within them, the more specific conflicts of institutional missions, types of students, disciplinary versus interdisciplinary, paradigm versus narrative, faculty versus administrative roles, on- versus off-campus contributions, and public versus private life issues.

Undergraduate Study Identifications

- Did you choose courses based on subject matter or the faculty who taught them?

- Recall two or three faculty members whom you admired. In what ways did you learn from them? How did they give you feedback about the quality of your work?

- How did faculty members demonstrate their scholarly expertise and thinking to you?

- Did they stimulate you to think on your own? Using theoretical material? Sophisticated discovery methods? Practical applications? Connections with other fields?

- Did you think of them, *then*, as teachers or as scholars? *Now?*
- Why did you choose the major field or professional area of your baccalaureate?
- What were your experiences of learning to write in your major field?
- What were the conflicts in balancing academic studies, family, work, and leisure? Looking back, what seems out of balance?
- Describe the most significant turning point(s) in your under-graduate years.

Graduate or Professional School Foundations

- How and why did you choose a place for graduate/professional study?
- What was the prevailing ethos among graduate students—com-petition or collaboration? Among the faculty—hierarchical or collegial? What was the quality of relationships among graduate students? Between graduate students and the faculty?
- Did you have a mentor(s)? Describe their qualities and their limitations.
- How did you learn about delivering conference papers? About publishing in refereed journals or book chapters? About grant applications and their management?
- What did you know about the strengths and limitations of your department chair? Dean of your college? President of the institution?
- Was any faculty member with whom you worked involved in gov-ernance of the organizations of your field? Did they do editorial work and get you involved in these professional activities?
- How did you manage the unrelenting pressure to be in the library/lab/field versus having a personal life? What felt out of balance?
- Describe the most significant turning point(s) in your graduate student years.

Entry Into Academic Life and Early Career Issues

- When you began as an assistant professor, what did you under-stand to be the institutional/program priorities for your teaching, scholarship, and service? How did your understanding change during your probationary period?

- Did you have a plan for developing your pedagogy when you started?
- Describe your most vivid recollection(s) of teaching during your probationary period.
- When and how did you develop a philosophy of teaching—a schema—that went beyond being knowledgeable of subject matter and attuned to daily classroom dynamics?
- Did you have an explicit research plan for the first five years, a step-by-step description of scholarly projects?
- Describe how you launched your research program. Did you include students, graduate or undergraduate, in these projects?
- Did you attempt to secure internal or external funding for your scholarship? What did you learn most from that process? Was the application or funding rewarded?
- What were your first publication experiences and what did you learn from that process?
- Did you have a mentor(s) as an assistant professor? What was the nature of that relationship and what were its benefits and costs?
- What was the quality of relationships among the junior and senior members of the department? Was it a competitive or a collegial environment?
- What expectations did other faculty have for your participation on committees in the department, college, or university?
- Were you encouraged to participate in your disciplinary or professional association or learned society? To volunteer for editorial tasks in the journals or on grant review panels?
- How did you balance the proportions of time spent on teaching, scholarship, and service? On professional pursuits on and off campus?
- What was out of proportion and what short- and longer-range consequences did it have?

- What was the most significant decision(s) you made about academic life during this probationary period? What were its consequences?
- Did you ever consider changing institutions as an assistant professor?

Post-Tenure and Mid-Career Issues

- Did you have a specific plan for post-tenure academic life? Becoming a full professor?
- What goals did you set for your continuing development as a teacher? What was working the best in your strategies? Did you experiment with new strategies or continue what seemed to be working pretty well?
- How often did you change your syllabi? Develop new courses?
- Who were the students with whom you worked particularly well? Who were most difficult or disappointing? What comments on student evaluations gave you the most cause for concern?
- How did you know that your students knew what you wanted them to know?
- What aspects of your philosophy of teaching or its strategies did you believe were most appreciated and most misunderstood by students or other faculty members in the department?
- How did you think differently about your research program after promotion and tenure? Did you see the promotion as an opportunity to change directions?
- How did your committee assignments change after tenure? Did you participate in faculty governance? Were you asked to be chair of department, college, or university committees? Were you able to bring your teaching or scholarly expertise to bear in committee work?
- Did you have an expectation for how you wanted your department, college, or campus trajectory to change when you became a vested stakeholder in its future?

- How did you think about participation in governance or editorial service in your area of expertise? Did you pursue them? What were your experiences of the costs and benefits of this work off campus to your reputation and respect on campus?

- After tenure, how well did you balance academic and professional pursuits, personal relationships, family commitments, and leisure activities?

- What was your awareness of and actual level of health during this time? What caused you the most sleepless nights?

- What was in and/or out of balance during this period? Were there any significant life events (e.g., death of a parent, death of a colleague, divorce, child's medical problems, etc.) that shifted your priorities and balancing strategies? How did you fare? What did you learn? What could you have managed more effectively?

- Looking back, what were your finest accomplishments of this period? Serious setbacks and disappointments? What did you learn from them?

- Did you ever grow bored with academic life and consider another career?

- What was the most significant understanding(s) of academic life and the professoriate that you took away from this period?

Later Stages of Academic Life

Imagine that your name appeared (quite prematurely) last week in the Death Notices section of *The Chronicle of Higher Education* or the flagship journal of your specialty area.

- Who would be asked to compose your obituary?

- What would they say about your teaching, your scholarship, and your citizenship to campus and the professional field?

- What would they say about your reputation with your colleagues, your personal friends, your students, and in your community?

- As you reflect on the elements that might be included, what gives you the most pride? In teaching? Scholarship? Citizenship in many and diverse communities?

- What was missing or misunderstood in your colleagues' synopses of your academic career and personal life?

- Are you wistful or saddened by what you read? Why does it matter? What would you modify, even slightly, if you could? Why don't you?

- Are you contented by what you read? Can you savor the affirmation by others and the confirmation of what you tried and sometimes succeeded beyond expectations?

- How did you plan to spend time during retirement? After the welter of assigned responsibilities dwindled? Was your intellectual and emotional life still vibrant?

- What was your new balance as you composed the concluding chapters of an academic life story?

- Given the opportunity—a last lecture—what message(s) would you want to communicate about academic life to others?

Conclusion

I first encountered the *Spiritual Exercises* of Saint Ignatius Loyola (Ganss, 1991) many years ago as a Fordham University undergraduate. Their structured form of reflection and self-evaluation were ideal stimuli and a respite from busy days filled with striving and sometimes accomplishing. More recently, my good friend and a distinguished psychologist worked with a spiritual director to do those exercises at Saint Louis University. I talked with him and others as I reflected on the etymologies of *profess, professor, vocation,* and *education.* Ours is a way of life that values insightful probing followed by truth-telling. We expect it of ourselves. We teach its traditions to our students.

Academics work very hard. We think deeply about the merits of our teaching, scholarship, and service, but also obsess about our limitations or insufficiencies. We chafe at nagging demands to construct dossiers to satisfy others' need for accountability. Too often, those repetitious demands to shine flashlights on our work carry with them an implicit message from the administrator, regent, or legislator—"We don't think you are working very hard, or hard enough to justify your salary, job security, and all of the unobserved and independent activities that characterize academic life." For the more senior faculty member, there is also the sentiment that significant resources are set aside for promising new faculty members versus rewarding the steady excellence of the long-term teacher, scholar, and citizen.

I tried to offer an antidote to such externally driven scripts that shoehorn our lives into neat sound-bite packages. Silko (1981) captured the vibrancy of oral tradition in this way: "The storyteller keeps the stories. . . . With these stories we will survive" (p. 247). Behar (2003) wrote, "We are storytellers with Ph.D.s and academic jobs. . . . We are chroniclers of the historical moment in which it has been our destiny to be thinkers" (pp. xvi–xvii). I recommend that faculty members use the prompts in this chapter to compose their stories and, in doing so, to cherish their valuable work.

Have you ever felt the energy in a room filled with academics as they remembered and shared stories about students, discoveries, colleagues, administrators, and thus, about themselves?

ACKNOWLEDGMENTS

I thank Allan Brawley and James Korn for their helpful commentaries on earlier versions of this chapter. They are two colleagues who always made the questions in my academic life so much easier to ask directly and honestly.

REFERENCES

Behar, R. (2003). Foreword. In D. P. Freedman & O. Frey (Eds.), *Autobiographical writing across the disciplines: A reader* (pp. xiii–xviii). Durham, NC: Duke University Press.

Bellah, R. N., Madsen, R., Sullivan, W. M., Swidler, A., & Tipton, S. M. (1985). *Habits of the heart: Individualism and commitment in American life.* Berkeley, CA: University of California Press.

Erikson, E. H., & Erikson, J. M. (1997). *The life cycle completed* (Extended version). New York, NY: Norton.

Ganss, G. E. (Ed.). (1991). *Ignatius of Loyola: The spiritual exercises and selected works.* Mahwah, NJ: Paulist Press.

Korn, J. H. (2002). Beyond tenure: The teaching portfolio for reflection and change. In S. F. Davis & W. Buskist (Eds.), *The teaching of psychology: Essays in honor of Wilbert J. McKeachie and Charles L. Brewer* (pp. 203–213). Mahwah, NJ: Lawrence Erlbaum.

McAdams, D. P. (1996). Personality, modernity, and the storied self: A contemporary framework for studying persons. *Psychological Inquiry, 7*(4), 295–321.

McAdams, D. P. (2001). The psychology of life stories. *Review of General Psychology, 5*(2), 100–122.

McAdams, D. P., & Logan, R. L. (2004). What is generativity? In E. de St. Aubin, D. P. McAdams, & T-C. Kim (Eds.), *The generative society: Caring for future generations* (pp. 15–31). Washington, DC: American Psychological Association.

Seldin, P. (2004). *The teaching portfolio: A practical guide to improved performance and promotion/tenure decisions* (3rd ed.). Bolton, MA: Anker.

Silko, L. M. (1981). *Storyteller.* New York, NY: Arcade.

Teaching Portfolios

Monica A. Devanas

8

A teaching portfolio is a collection of materials that describes and documents a faculty member's teaching effectiveness. It is meant to be eight to ten pages in length and supported by actual course materials, examples of student work, and assessments of teaching such as student ratings and peer review reports presented in an appendix. Most importantly, it includes a statement of the faculty member's teaching responsibilities, accomplishments as a teacher, and a self-reflection on his or her teaching philosophy.

One portion of the portfolio is a description of the teaching responsibilities of the faculty member. This description is more than phrases in the course catalogue. It provides details about the content of the courses taught, the types of students they are designed for, the teaching strategies used, and any additional information about the uniqueness of the courses and the professor's commitment to student learning embodied in them.

An instructor's teaching philosophy is a vital part of the teaching portfolio. Here, faculty describe their reasons for becoming a teacher, their reasons for teaching the way that they do, and the motivation for their teaching. A faculty member's statements on teaching may not obviously convey his or her teaching philosophy, so it is useful to think of this section as providing the rationale for one's teaching style, choice of assignments, and methods of assessment. In some cases a teaching philosophy may be difficult to articulate or even identify. It may be useful for the faculty member to analyze his or her course materials, assignments, and tests to examine the reasons for each, and to analyze the format to find a teaching method that defines the core principle for his or her teaching philosophy. For example, having many interactive group discussions in a course design may reveal the faculty member's commitment to active learning principles. Asking students to apply information to solve problems reveals a teaching philosophy grounded in the development of higher-order thinking skills.

The last section of the portfolio is the evidence section, which contains materials that document teaching effectiveness. Brief descriptions of materials are included in the body of this section, while the actual artifacts, which may be lengthy, are included in an appendix following the textual descriptions. Typical types of course-related documents that faculty include are course syllabi, assignments, examples of quizzes and exams, reading lists, and discussion questions. Faculty may also add results of student ratings surveys, if available.

The evidence section should contain documents or evidence from sources other than the faculty member. Peer observation reports, notes or email messages from students, and alumni surveys are all valuable sources. In some cases faculty may include letters or comments from colleagues who have visited their classes or reviewed curricular materials. Brief discussions of faculty development initiatives, such as conferences and workshops attended, may also be included if the teaching strategies learned or changes made to improve teaching as a result of participation are provided. It is very important to include such statements regarding the lessons learned and the teaching improvements that were made. A mere list of dates and topics does little to convince any reader that teaching methods have changed for the better. The strength and usefulness of the teaching portfolio in documenting teaching effectiveness relies on the inclusion of various kinds of evidence that support the faculty member's claim of being an effective teacher.

Why Are Teaching Portfolios Useful?

Teaching portfolios have a variety of purposes (Murray, 1997; Wright, Knight, & Pomerleau, 1999). For faculty, the portfolio is a way to organize and present their teaching record and accomplishments. In preparing materials for a teaching portfolio there is an opportunity for self-reflection on the practice of teaching that is a rare opportunity for most faculty members. The process of self-reflection has the outcome of making at least one fundamental change in one's practice. For example, faculty may never think about teaching the same way again, or they may recognize that even good practice can be improved, or they may become more aware of their teaching day to day. The power of the reflective process is quite transformative. Once faculty begin thinking about the how and why of their teaching (e.g., what is it that they value in their teaching and their students' learning, what strategies and methods they use for these outcomes, how they might have changed their teaching style over time), they will become more aware of their own effectiveness.

Complexity of Teaching and Individuality of Teaching

Since each person is unique, it follows that every portfolio is a unique representation of one person's individual style, methods, choice of content, and how these characteristics coalesce into an effective teacher. The act of teaching is a synthesis of a remarkable number of skills. A teacher needs to be writer, producer, director, actor, and critic simultaneously. One's own academic discipline, the reasons for seeing value in that area of study, and the passion and excitement of scholarly work in that subject, all distinctly influence how one teaches. Add to these characteristics the individual personality traits, style, and strength of communication skills and it is easy to see that each teacher, each person, is unique in his or her approach to teaching. Given all the activities and outcomes that can be assessed in one's teaching (Theall & Centra, 2001), the portfolio is the only tool robust enough to capture these attributes and combine them into a coherent whole.

The teaching portfolio is structured to allow faculty to describe the unique circumstances of their courses and their approaches and motivations for teaching in general as well as their use of specific strategies and methods and why they are effective.

Uses of Teaching Portfolios

It is very important to consider the purpose for which the portfolio is to be used. This purpose will significantly affect the arrangement of materials and how they are described as evidence to document teaching. Developing a teaching portfolio allows the faculty member to connect theory with practice, provides an opportunity to evidence claims of effectiveness, and grounds the discussion in factual documentation. Professors by definition are seekers of truth. Thus, when a faculty member begins this kind of self-reflection and self-assessment, there is a natural outcome of improvement, as one is no longer satisfied with the status quo.

Personal Improvement

Many new faculty programs suggest that junior faculty begin collecting the information and evidence needed for a teaching portfolio, since this material will ultimately be used for future personnel decisions. However, many programs are now inviting faculty to create teaching portfolios for personal improvement. In some cases entire schools or departments have embraced the initiative and find there is a richer context for discussions on teaching and an overall trend to improved instruction by all faculty.

If the teaching portfolio is to be used for personal assessment, then the collection of formative materials, suggestions for improvements, personal concerns, and challenges of the faculty member may be very important for the broad overview of teaching performance.

This activity evokes Palmer's (1998) definition of teaching as being the most public and the most private thing we do. A faculty member so engaged can easily find areas where he or she may need improvement and can set specific short-term and long-term objectives. For personal use and self-improvement, certain types of materials may be the focus of examination such as student comments and suggestions of peer review committees. These same items would not be the center of any collection of materials to be used in a portfolio developed for a public purpose such as a personnel decision. In public instances, portfolio materials are more like those of an artist or architect in that the best works are being used to evidence success and effectiveness in teaching.

Personnel Decisions

Most faculty members first consider developing a teaching portfolio when they are required to provide hard evidence with specific data about their own teaching effectiveness for reappointment or tenure or promotion decisions. At this career point it is important to focus on the components and evidence that demonstrate and document the professor's best work in teaching and that indicate students are successful in their individual course assignments, courses of study, and careers. The faculty member's achievements, awards, and successes are the focus. Materials to highlight include new courses, new instructional initiatives, and grants for supporting the creation of new courses. Course descriptions should showcase the multiple opportunities for learning by all students and their successful outcomes. The documents themselves do not change, but the priority and value given to their description and discussion must attend to the purpose. Self-criticism is a key component in the portfolio developed for personal improvement, but it is not a strong point for argument when one is being considered for tenure.

Additionally, it is very important for any faculty member submitting a teaching portfolio for a personnel decision to consider the readers. Administrators and department officers are likely reviewers of portfolio packets. Some may have had extensive experience with portfolios, while others may not (Centra, 2000). It is clearly an advantage to have an organized collection of materials, well tabulated and cross-referenced, so that the valuable time of the review committee is not wasted looking for evidence. It is highly advisable that the preface or first page of the portfolio include an executive summary or list of critical activities so that high-priority contributions and highly valued accomplishments in teaching are obvious and easy to find.

Awards

When the portfolio is submitted as part of an application for a teaching award, the strategies are similar to those used for personnel decisions. The focus needs to be on the valued accomplishments. Student comments, letters, and products can illustrate effectiveness better than anything the candidate might write. Likewise, peer reviews and comments from colleagues are very strong recommendations for award applications. Be sure the contributions for teaching that are specifically noted for the award, such as a science course for non-majors, are well marked and documented.

New Positions

If the portfolio is to be used as part of an application for a new position, it should include the activities that mark this candidate as superior. It may be his or her ability to create new courses to support areas for curricular development within a discipline, or his or her success in reaching out to other departments and implementing interdisciplinary courses. It is critical that the teaching portfolio connect the candidate's achievements to the needs of the department with the open position. Having a record of successful teaching that is evidenced by syllabi, course materials, and assignments and includes glowing student comments and instructional ratings makes a very strong case for a new faculty position candidate.

Legacy

Some senior faculty members develop portfolios as they approach retirement. Their purpose is to document their lengthy careers as a legacy to the department. Many wonderful historical reflections about the institution, discipline, changes in student body, and tools for teaching are captured and annotated for others to appreciate.

For What Audience?

Self

If the teaching portfolio is to remain a personal, private document seen only by the faculty member, then the collection of materials, notes, reflections, and comments may be in whatever order or form suits the individual. However, once the process is started, it would be advantageous to bring the portfolio to a level of organization that would allow it to be shared with others.

Colleagues

Occasionally department chairs have completed portfolios to model the process for their faculty. This experience helps chairs understand the challenges of developing a teaching portfolio (especially if many years of records need to be documented), the need for faculty to rigorously document their claims for effectiveness, and the fact that assessment of teaching is based on evidence.

Review Committees

When review committees are the primary readers of a teaching portfolio, it is best to keep the organization simple and easy to follow, with specific references from the narrative sections to the appendix materials. An executive summary of the most outstanding accomplishments is a great help to harried reviewers. Bulleted lists of courses or tables that include courses and the years they were taught also help to present a long and varied teaching record in a small space with major impact.

Materials to Be Included in the Teaching Portfolio

There are many types of information and documentation that can be used in a teaching portfolio. It is important to note that there should be a balance of material from multiple sources. Ideally, information from the professor, such as course descriptions, a reflective statement, and course materials, is supplemented with documentation by students, peers, and colleagues in other departments or institutions. Student products, in the form of essays, exams, and research projects, support and verify the claims of a particular type of teaching or a level of achievement by the students. As noted by Seldin (2004), the following is a collection of suggested materials that should be included in a teaching portfolio.

Material From Oneself

- A statement of teaching responsibilities that includes course titles, numbers, enrollments, and levels (e.g., graduate or undergraduate, upper-level or introductory, required for the major, elective, or service)
- A teaching philosophy or reflective statement that describes the faculty member's personal commitment to teaching, strategies and objectives, methods, expected learning outcomes, individual motivations for teaching, and how and why one teaches
- Representative course syllabi that describe course content, learning objectives, course projects, readings, and homework assignments
- New courses or curriculum revisions, course assignments, projects, materials, or pedagogical innovations, such as moving from

a lecture-based form of course delivery to group discussions and team projects

- New course materials that may have been developed, including case studies, course reading packets, study guides, laboratory manuals, innovative course projects or assignments, and activities such as service-learning opportunities

- Instructional modifications or innovations with measurements of their success, such as using videos in class, computer-enhanced course materials, or course web pages

- A description of efforts to improve teaching, such as participating in workshops or programs for instructional approaches or teaching development

- Research done on one's own teaching effectiveness or research that contributes to teaching, such as pre-tests and post-tests of student learning

- Grants to support or improve teaching, and any teaching awards

- Committee work relating to teaching in the department or institution, or national organizations in which teaching and learning improvement issues were the main focus

- Goals and plans for teaching for the next five years

Material From Others

- Student course or teaching evaluation data that indicate effectiveness or areas needing improvement

- Recognition, awards, or honors from students or colleagues, such as the dean's award for contributions or a student advising award

- Statements from peer review committees that conducted regular classroom visits as well as statements from colleagues who reviewed course materials, reading lists, assignments, and assessments

- A statement from the chairperson attesting to contributions made to department teaching or advising needs

- Documentation of efforts to develop teaching through participation in programs offered by the campus center for teaching and learning

- Invitations from outside the faculty member's institution to be a guest speaker or present a paper at a conference on teaching

- Statements from colleagues about program design and materials and online instruction

- Comments from colleagues and students on the clarity and meaningfulness of the advising process

- Letters or emails from graduates detailing their appreciation of instructional quality, professional preparation, or advising

- Comments or letters from colleagues at other institutions remarking on the quality of preparation of students for graduate studies

- Indication of assistance given to colleagues with course or program design, study materials or teaching methods, or mentoring junior faculty as they develop teaching skills

Products of Good Teaching and Student Learning

- Student pre-test and post-test scores indicating effective teaching and learning

- Student journals, essays, field journals, laboratory notebooks, and self-studies on learning

- Examples of graded student assignments detailing the faculty member's effort to guide and direct student development of critical thinking or written communication skills

- Several examples of graded student work that represents different levels of quality: excellent, good, average

- Successive drafts of student work showing improvement in quality as a result of the faculty member's comments and guidance

- Collections of materials that show student learning over time, such as from the beginning and end of a course or program of study

- Student conference presentations or published writings based on course-related work with guidance by and support from the faculty member

- Awards won by students in course- or discipline-based competitions, such as model business development or design competitions

- Comments from students indicating appreciation of guidance on career development or assistance in obtaining employment or entrance into graduate school

- A record of students who have succeeded in advanced study or professional accomplishments

How Should the Teaching Portfolio Be Constructed?

Much of the information that makes up a teaching portfolio is prepared by the faculty member— descriptions of courses, reflections on teaching, and collection of evidence. But the portfolio should not be developed in isolation. It is best done in collaboration with a mentor or colleague who can provide feedback on the clarity of materials, the possible connections between statements in the philosophy and course activities and assignments, other activities related to teaching, or an objective opinion regarding claims and supporting evidence. Ideally, a mentor should be involved in the portfolio development process from the beginning. It is best if the mentor is outside the faculty member's department or discipline so that discussions stay focused on important objectives such as the goals for creating the teaching portfolio, the information that will be collected, and how it will be analyzed and presented. A good mentor will guide the process, relying on his or her own wide knowledge of teaching assessment and procedures, alternative formats for many evaluation practices, and value in teaching practices. A good mentor provides an objective review of the narrative and supporting materials as well as encouragement as the faculty member struggles with creating the portfolio.

Although many faculty would like to take weeks, if not months, to create a portfolio, Seldin (2004) notes that it is best accomplished by dedicating blocks of time over several days and may take most faculty 12 to 15 hours, even if they are working with a skilled mentor.

Steps to Prepare a Teaching Portfolio

There are some logical steps to preparing a teaching portfolio. Begin by planning the process. Consider the purpose, the readers, the kinds of evidence that will be important and where to find it. Then summarize all teaching responsibilities by describing courses, their content and levels, learning goals and objectives, the teaching strategies used, and special assignments or innovations. If many years of teaching or many different courses are to be described, a table containing the courses and the semesters they were taught in is an easy and quick way to represent the many teaching responsibilities that a professor may have had even over a few short years. All aspects of teaching are included: advising, sponsoring student groups, supervising graduate students, and teaching staff.

The next step is to describe the why of one's teaching. This is the teaching philosophy section and should contain such information as beliefs about teaching (e.g., students should be actively engaged), goals (e.g., students should develop a critical ability to analyze texts for historical value), and strategies (e.g., reading primary sources connects students with the richness of the research in the discipline). Next, consider the materials to be collected and prepare statements describing each item (e.g., syllabi, course reading assignments, group projects, and assessments). Once collected, the items are arranged in order, typically in a three-ring binder with tabs clearly separating sections. Portfolios should be revised as frequently as a curriculum vitae.

There is a growing interest in using electronic formats for teaching portfolios (see Kahn, 2004). Many faculty find it easy to make links between their online portfolio documents and web-based course materials, syllabi, and student projects. Having a digital or online teaching portfolio is an advantage if a professor is seeking another position or looking to share this information with colleagues at other institutions. But for most traditional faculty assessment needs, such as tenure or promotion, a hardcopy of the portfolio, presented in a binder and containing the supporting materials and an appendix, is still the preferred format for most institutional internal review processes.

If you are creating a portfolio for personnel decisions, focus on your best work. Be sure to reinforce statements about teaching methods and strategies with evidence of successful student learning as a result of those methods, student comments indicating their recognition of learning via those methods, and concurrence by peers and colleagues whenever possible. The following is a suggested table of contents for a portfolio used for promotion (Seldin, 2004):

TEACHING PORTFOLIO

Name of Faculty Member

Institution

Department/College

Date

Table of Contents
1) Teaching Responsibilities
2) Teaching Philosophy
3) Teaching Objectives, Strategies, and Methods
4) Student Evaluation Ratings
   • Table of data from summative questions
   • Overall teaching effectiveness

- All courses over time
- Provide complete collection of data in appendix

5) Peer Review Reports of Classroom Observation

6) Representative Course Syllabi With Annotations

7) Evidence of Student Learning With Student Products

8) Review of Teaching Materials by Colleagues

9) Teaching Awards

10) Short-Term and Long-Term Teaching Goals

11) Appendixes

In other formats and with emphasis on formative materials, a teaching portfolio that is used to improve teaching could include a list such as this (Seldin, 2004):

TEACHING PORTFOLIO

Name of Faculty Member

Institution

Department/College

Date

Table of Contents

1)   Teaching Responsibilities

2)   Teaching Philosophy

3)   Teaching Objectives, Strategies, and Methods

4)   Student Evaluation Ratings

- Table of data from formative questions
- Teaching areas needing improvement
- All courses over time
- Provide complete collection of data in appendix

5) Description of Teaching Materials
   - Syllabi
   - Assignments
   - Projects
6) Efforts to Improve Teaching
   - Teaching conferences and workshops attended
   - New methods learned and incorporated into instruction
   - Innovations in teaching and curricular design
   - Revisions of courses, incorporation of web-based learning tools
7) Comments From Teaching Center Staff on Classroom Observation
8) Evidence of Student Learning/Improvement With New Methods
9) Short-Term and Long-Term Teaching Goals
10) Appendixes

Suggestions for Teaching Portfolios

Strategies for Success

Creating a quality portfolio takes a great deal of time and energy. But this is well-invested effort, since almost all of the portfolio can be used for tenure and promotion decisions. The time spent finding and organizing materials during the portfolio writing process can be vastly shortened by keeping copies of course materials in a file folder or on a personal computer. To streamline the process of updating the portfolio at the end of each academic year, maintain a collection of materials from all courses taught during each semester. This allows for the easy addition of new materials (and deletion of old information) to keep the portfolio current and correct.

Faculty may find it useful to reflect on specific aspects of their teaching as they compose their teaching philosophy. Questions such as the following help faculty to see their purpose in teaching, their strengths and strategies, and the components that are part of one's teaching philosophy:

- What is your greatest strength as a teacher?
- What has been your most significant teaching accomplishment?
- How do you motivate superstar students?
- How do you motivate those who are struggling? (Seldin, 2004, pp. 13–14)
- If you overheard your students talking about you and your teaching in the cafeteria, what would they likely be saying? What would you like them to say? Why is this important to you? (Seldin, 1993, p. 21)

A successful portfolio presents a clear connection between teaching strategies and methods, teaching philosophy statements or themes, and documents used as evidence or support of teaching effectiveness. A model portfolio connects the primary principles of the teaching philosophy to course materials, descriptions of assignments, and comments from students and peers. The more connections there are between the central themes, the stronger the case is for successful teaching.

Mentors play a vital role in the teaching portfolio process (see Annis, 1993). A good mentor needs to be both a coach and a critic, someone who can motivate the faculty member while maintaining an objective perspective. A good mentor relationship might develop between a new or junior faculty member and a more senior professor, colleagues from different departments, or even a faculty development staff member.

Another important aspect to consider is the timeframe for writing the portfolio. The portfolio completion rate decreases compared to the time period over which the effort stretches. A dedicated, brief allotment of time, four to five days, is ideal for drafting a teaching portfolio with virtually complete supporting materials.

Institutional support is critical for faculty success in developing portfolios. The value and recognition of teaching by colleagues, the department, and the institution are important motivators for faculty to do their best work. Using the portfolio to present the individual, concise, factual, and robust record of teaching effectiveness improves teaching in the individual as well as across the institution.

Pitfalls to Avoid

Be aware of providing materials in an unbalanced proportion. Faculty often find that much of the information gathered for the portfolio comes from themselves (e.g., syllabi, course assignments, reading lists, discussion questions, lecture outlines, study guides). It is important that the portfolio reflect almost equal numbers of items from other contributions. Student surveys, student work, student ratings, comments from students, and notes from alumni are necessary to document that students were learning as the professor was teaching. The feedback from peer review reports, letters from the department chair following annual review meetings, and comments from colleagues who critiqued course designs or exam questions offer an objective perspective to the student products and collection of materials from the faculty member.

The portfolio is designed to be a reflection of the faculty member's teaching. As teaching assignments change, new strategies are incorporated and new resources are developed. The portfolio must be continuously updated to reflect changes in teaching. It is best to avoid the common pitfall of leaving the portfolio untouched once it is completed. Teaching is a dynamic activity, and the portfolio needs to mirror that fact. Annual updates are easy to accomplish if the faculty member has kept an organized, growing collection of data from the previous year. Additionally, a corollary pitfall is to update the portfolio with new, supporting material but to never remove the old material. The target size for a portfolio is eight to ten pages; in order to add new items, older items must be edited or removed.

Incentives for Faculty Participation

Faculty are extraordinarily busy people. Time is the most cherished commodity. Asking faculty to take the time to document their teaching will require great justification. Motivation in the form of special faculty development programs, recognition of the effort of creating a portfolio, or a token stipend for participation may be helpful in initiating an institutional portfolio program. Once a core group of faculty have created their own teaching portfolios, the initiative is likely to spread. These faculty have documented their accomplishments and achievements and are better prepared for competition for teaching awards as well as personnel decisions.

The teaching portfolio is a source of pride for most professors, and they willingly share it with others. Along with the intellectual engagement of colleagues, there is a connection to the primary motivation that all professors have for teaching—the love of the discipline and the desire to share that excitement of learning with others. A completed portfolio records a professor's success in the profession, and it is a well-accepted method for the evaluation and assessment of teaching.

There are several practical reasons why the portfolio process should be adopted by faculty and administrators. The teaching portfolio is a vehicle for self-reflection, dialogue, and transformation. Through self-study, faculty investigate their own teaching with the same rigor they use in their scholarship. Once created, the portfolio is a form or structure in which the unique collection of teaching accomplishments are described to colleagues, despite differences in modes of instruction, disciplines, or schools (Frost & Teodorescu, 2001). This rich, meaningful discussion of teaching can be a foundation for work on the scholarship of teaching. Faculty can better document the work that they do, and administrators can make more informed decisions about the future of their institutions. Ultimately, the teaching portfolio process becomes an initiative for continuous improvements in teaching and transforming the institution and the profession.

REFERENCES

Annis, L. F. (1993). The key role of the mentor. In P. Seldin, *Successful use of teaching portfolios* (pp. 19–25). Bolton, MA: Anker.

Centra, J. A. (2000). Evaluating the teaching portfolio: A role for colleagues. In K. E. Ryan (Ed.), *New directions for teaching and learning: Vol. 83. Evaluating teaching in higher education: A vision for the future* (pp. 87–93). San Francisco, CA: Jossey-Bass.

Frost, S. H., & Teodorescu, D. (2001, Summer). Teaching excellence: How faculty guided change at a research university. *Review of Higher Education, 24*(4), 397–415.

Kahn, S. (2004). Making good work public through electronic teaching portfolios. In P. Seldin, *The teaching portfolio: A practical guide to improved performance and promotion/tenure decisions* (3rd ed., pp. 36–50). Bolton, MA: Anker.

Murray, J. P. (1997). *Successful faculty development and evaluation: The complete teaching portfolio.* Washington, DC: Graduate School of Education and Human Development, The George Washington University. (ERIC Document Reproduction Service No. ED405759)

Palmer, P. J. (1998). *The courage to teach: Exploring the inner landscape of a teacher's life.* San Francisco, CA: Jossey-Bass.

Seldin, P. (1993). *Successful use of teaching portfolios.* Bolton, MA: Anker.

Seldin, P. (2004). *The teaching portfolio: A practical guide to improved performance and promotion/tenure decisions* (3rd ed.). Bolton, MA: Anker.

Theall, M., & Centra, J. A. (2001). Assessing the scholarship of teaching: Valid decisions from valid evidence. In C. Kreber (Ed.), *New directions for teaching and learning: Vol. 86. Scholarship revisited: Perspectives on the scholarship of teaching* (pp. 31–43). San Francisco, CA: Jossey-Bass.

Wright, W. A., Knight, P. T., & Pomerleau, N. (1999). Portfolio people: Teaching and learning dossiers and innovation in higher education. *Innovative Higher Education, 24*(2), 89–103.

Evaluating Faculty Research

Teck-Kah Lim

9

Each year, tens of thousands of college faculty have various facets of their professional lives placed under the microscope and evaluated. Perhaps the most important of these is the quality and productivity of their research. For the individual who has participated in such an exercise, either as the researcher under study or, on the other side of the lens, as the evaluator, it is obvious that research evaluation can be an inexact science. Most of the time it is both art and science. What is good? What is not so good? What is adequate? What is not? What should count? What should not? Answers to these questions usually depend on the evaluator. The process is in large measure a matter of perspective. If the protagonists belong to different disciplines or are groups rather than individuals, if the evaluator is the general public, these questions become even more problematic.

Is it because a stable checklist of primary indicators (performance measures) of research quality and productivity cannot be constructed? Must a checklist be customized each and every time? Or if such checklists do exist, is it a problem to evaluate and then respond to each item on the lists, or is it difficult to analyze and summarize the data that have been collected?

It is often all of these and, as a consequence, for most evaluators objective assessments of researchers (either individually or as a group) and their work can be difficult. Nevertheless, it is my premise that as long as evaluation methods are set up that account for the audience; the kind of researcher or group being evaluated; the type of outputs, outcomes, or impacts being measured; the period involved; and the environment in which the research is conducted, it is still possible to give some rigor and accountability to the process.

Thus it is my intent to explain these evaluation issues and how to react to them so as to make the best of what can be a sticky situation. This chapter will focus on what to do when one is called upon to evaluate a body of work over a period of time; it will only briefly discuss what to do when evaluating a particular piece of work.

To be a fair-minded and educated evaluator, it is necessary to appreciate what research is, to consider the human element in it, to know its form and practice, and to place it in the context of the mission of an institution. Then one must have a reasonable idea of its actual practice in different disciplines. What are the behavior patterns, what are the mores, what are the cultures of a particular group of researchers? Only after having conducted this anthropological study can anyone possibly attempt reliable assessments and evaluations.

Research Defined

A generally accepted definition of research is the process of creating new knowledge or of making discoveries. It is exploration or "searching out" at the frontiers of current knowledge to expand our understanding of a subject. It can be the synthesis of existing knowledge to reveal new insights and solutions to unsolved problems. In short, it is the process of making an original intellectual or creative contribution.

More specifically, it is the English professor trying to authenticate Shakespearean manuscripts, the economist seeking possible correlations between flirtatious women MBAs and their promotion prospects, the climatologist deciphering temperature changes over eons to decide if global warming is taking place, the epidemiologist predicting the progress of avian flu, Einstein developing the theory of relativity. Some research is said to be basic—Is there another solar system planet beyond Pluto?—with little immediate economic impact. Some produces an immediate benefit, as when scientists develop a new drug for a disease.

By and large, any research, even without immediate realizable benefit, just through its inexorable march to new knowledge is worthwhile (if we avoid cost-effectiveness issues) and in totality with other work always leads to innovation and economic growth. Consider, for example, lasers and the Internet, and before them X-rays. That's not to deny that on occasion one does not sit up and wonder why some faculty member is studying the way a piece of toast falls to the ground: Does it land buttered-side up? As Byrne (1990) has remarked, research in the ivory tower can be fuzzy, irrelevant, and pretentious. Fortunately, it is possible to tell what is serious and what is frivolous. One just has to ask the question—What is its purpose?—and diligently work out the answer. It is also clear that the constant questioning and the search for answers that is integral to research can play a vital role in the life of the mind and can be trained to address local, national, and global problems.

If research can be defined as the search to know, must that label be restricted only to activities in the third party? That is, must the researcher be studying an area, an issue, as a disengaged observer? Is a teacher who is studying his or her own practices—questioning (Is a web-based course more effective in bringing about learning than face-to-face lectures?), exploring, devising a strategy, executing it, testing, analyzing the results, and sharing them (e.g., through course portfolios)—not doing scholarly research? Indeed, Ernest Boyer (1990), Eugene Rice (1996), and Lee Shulman (2000), among others, have claimed that these activities constitute the scholarship of teaching and sit under the big tent of educational research. Provided the professor has invested the intellectual powers normally associated with traditional research into the work, has he or she not met the strictures of credibility, and does the work not deserve the stamp of scholarship?

The Role of Research in a College or University

If an objective of the institution is to help shape the societal agenda, research can provide a means for faculty service to the community. To be sure, there are other more intrinsic values to research at the university or college. It is a given that teaching and research are inseparable in today's institutions; they enhance one another. The primary goal of the professoriate is to educate the mind, not only of its students but itself as well. Research forces the practitioner to be inquisitive and to cast a fresh look at things, which can add an extra dimension to a professor's teaching. It is often claimed, without any perceived need for justification, that what is research today is part of a standard text tomorrow, so a professor had better be prepared. It may also be said that when institutions allow faculty to do research, it keeps them happy in their "playpen." If faculty were forced to only teach, all colleges and universities would lose the services of a majority of their best brains.

Research has the capacity for major results, and reputations are made through discoveries that catch the eye and attention of the public. Thus institutions realize that status and ranking hinge on it. The better the reputation and the higher the prestige, the easier it is to attract students and extramural funding. Research is a value-added activity and takes its place near the head of the line in the mission of many colleges and universities. At research universities, so labeled because of the predominance of research being conducted at these campuses, it has also given rise to an industry: the training of graduate students to be the new acolytes of the professoriate and the research enterprise.

The Practice of Research

Differences in the nature of knowledge from one discipline to another engender different cultures that in turn effect differences in how research is practiced in any setting. In the sciences, new knowledge is built atop the old. There is a natural progression and an obvious linkage among before, now, and after. Wasn't it Newton who said that if he saw far at all, it was because he stood on the shoulders of others? Any discovery of research in science, in the main, is not a revolution. For any significant problem, there is usually a race to find the solution, and there is a definite winner who takes all. Thus the claim for priority places extreme pressure on every research scientist who does not labor in the backwaters of his or her area. On the other hand, scholarly work in the humanities (scholarly being used advisedly as a reminder that many people wish to distinguish the predominant activity of analysis and interpretation that permeates almost all humanities work from the discovery-oriented activity in the sciences) does not develop out of previous work. The new in the humanities very often is a bolt from out of the blue. As Eugene Garfield (1980), founder of Science Citation Index, so succinctly put it,

> . . . if you are a music scholar preparing a monograph on Bach and a book on the composer comes out, you are of course interested, but you do not burn your manuscript. You know that no one (including yourself) will ever be able to say the last word about Bach and his music. (p. 43)

Priority is of less concern in the humanities.

Another difference is glaringly obvious between research in the sciences and the humanities. For example, modern science is largely a team-oriented, laboratory-based activity, so research scientists usually work in groups on a common, broad research goal. Between the demands of the team and the objective of priority, it is not stretching the truth too much to say that the life of the typical active researcher in the sciences is frenetic, with whirring machines to be attended to and data to be collected. Science research can demand 24/7 commitment; in many areas it is invariably a young person's sport. Thus the common wisdom is that research scientists wither with age, their bright ideas peter out earlier. They can keep up their frenetic pace for only so long; eventually they lose touch and become outdated.

Research in the humanities, however, is more solitary and by comparison more sedentary and slow-paced. It relies mainly on writing, reading, understanding, and interpretation, not on discovery. Students start later, take longer to finish, and rarely serve as apprentices to professors. For them, working in large teams is not the norm. The humanist can grow wiser with age.

In the sciences and engineering, the ability to bring a large team together can spell the difference between being able to do the work or not. Thus recruiting is an important facet of science research. Large teams are necessary because the machines they use for research need many hands; they are, incidentally, also expensive to purchase and maintain. The ability to find coworkers (mostly graduate students) and to fund them—while science and engineering graduate students receive stipends and tuition remission, the humanist enjoys no such luxury—is of paramount importance for any enterprising science researcher. To snare them from the competition, to keep his or her charges focused and willing to put in the long hours at the work bench, the science professor, more so than a counterpart in humanities, has to be a good mentor, be perceived to have good standing in the field, and be doing exciting forefront research. These "groupies" must want to be connected to the laboratory of that professor because there aren't better rewards elsewhere. The researcher's role as master, teacher, advisor, and even trusted friend can continue beyond each trainee's graduation. Thus the mentor can often claim credit for his or her charge's success in the future.

Because research requires an investment of resources that is often beyond the means of the university, every faculty member engaged in research is expected to seek outside sources of funds. In some fields, such as the humanities, social sciences, and business, few sources exist for research support; in others, such as science, medicine, and engineering, research dollars are more easily available. In almost every field, faculty must compete sometimes against the best in the world to get these outside dollars. There are three main sources of these funds: government, foundations, and industry. Any time the researcher wishes to pry loose dollars from one of these entities, he or she must submit a proposal with a great idea and a compelling program of work. Insofar as the need for funds is greater for the scientist, a significant chunk of time must be devoted to preparing these proposals. Some (the super professors) succeed beyond their wildest dreams and, with funds aplenty, are able to run teams that number more than a handful.

An idea that does not find public expression contributes nothing to our general knowledge. It cannot be criticized and tested and it therefore cannot contribute to the discourse that moves our understanding of that area forward. Recognizing that, we demand that research, to be considered meaningful, must produce a publication or a public expression of results that can be reviewed and understood by others. It can involve an article in a journal (usually called a paper), an exhibit in a gallery or a juried show, a book for general audiences, a poem in a magazine or anthology, or a presentation at a conference. Whatever the form, dissemination is an essential component of the research effort. The researcher also needs to publicize his work since that is crucial to recruiting and securing priority for his idea.

For researchers, the most recognized and the most traditional of channels to disseminate their work is peer-reviewed journals, especially those that are influential and widely read. These possess impact capability (e.g., *Nature, Science, Journal of the American Medical Association, New England Journal of Medicine*, among the science journals) and have cachet conferred on them by virtue of their strict refereeing and distinguished record of publishing—the best works are published there. However, the considerable length of time expended in writing the paper and getting it accepted through a peer review process forces researchers to be smart about finding the right journal for their work. If they believe what they have discovered is really significant and that timeliness of publication is an overriding consideration, they may trim back the size of the paper and look to those journals that just accept letters (shortened papers) so that the work can be made public immediately or as soon as possible. This imperative raises the standard for refereeing, and when a researcher's manuscript finds acceptance by the letters journal it casts a halo around the work.

Many humanities researchers eschew journals; they prefer books. They are less compulsive about the literature than scientists are—another outgrowth of the difference between scientific research and humanistic scholarship.

It must also be realized that publication patterns and rates between the humanities and the sciences differ. Mathematicians and business professors publish fewer papers than chemistry professors, though they may make up for that by greater page count per paper. In regard to the need for dissemination, another complication has surfaced recently: Researchers are also publishing in electronic journals, an activity that is catching on and for which attitudes are still forming.

Just as there are would-be authors seeking a vehicle to publicize their work or would-be grantees looking for support, there must be referees who act as gatekeepers to ensure that only quality papers are accepted and quality proposals are funded. When a researcher becomes known for his or her contributions to an area or if their work is cited in an article or proposal that has been submitted, the researcher is often called upon to review it. This is another responsibility of the good-citizen researcher—the collective burden of helping to keep the area "clean," thriving, and nurturing. This obligation is made lighter by the fact that an invitation to referee is really an accolade, a tip of the hat by the editors or program managers that you are visibly qualified as an expert. If the researcher's good citizenship and intellectual talents are matched by leadership and organizational skills, he or she may even be tapped to help run the professional society for his or her discipline or be the convener of a conference.

With the appearance of team-driven research, there is the problem of multi-authored papers. Single-authored papers are now a rarity while papers in particle physics can have 120 "fathers" in the byline. With so many coauthors how is one able to disentangle the contribution of each? There are no defined criteria for determining authorship. Some are "earned" because the researcher has contributed significantly to the work, others are "honorary," where the researcher's name is included because he directs the group doing the work or has assisted on routine technical aspects of the project or has found the funding to carry it out. Though discouraged, the latter practice still survives. Unless one knows the group dynamics intimately, the type of authorship to be assigned to the individual researcher can only be surmised. Will two two-author papers be equivalent to one single-author publication? Is the authorship order significant? What are the norms? Various traditions are espoused. In some laboratories, the senior professor is the last-named author while the researcher who did the most work among the others is named first. In others, the senior professor takes pride of place at the head of the line no matter what. In others still, the names are in alphabetical order irrespective of the extent of actual contribution. An evaluator has to determine which method was used.

Researchers often talk about their work at conferences, and most of these are open to all paid registrants. Less value should then be attached to attendance and participation in their poster sessions. However, an invited presentation at a plenary session reflects recognition of worth or standing by the conveners.

In the process of writing papers and presenting talks, researchers acknowledge or credit the contributions of others and do so by citing the work upon which they draw; the norms of research oblige its adherents to do so. It follows, then, that if a work is cited, it must be deemed useful and thus the number of citations may be regarded as a measure of the usefulness, impact, or influence of the article or presentation. Access to this data is now easier with the advent of Science Citation Index and other indexes. However, a piece of work may be cited so as to identify methodology, provide background reading to place the work in context, correct flaws, or just to authenticate data; it provides useful background literature and no more. The evaluator must sniff this out.

Science research remembers little of old information so citations of a particular paper have a limited lifetime. This is not so for the humanities, where an article can slowly gain citations for a long time. Also, because many humanities publications are books, it is much more challenging to track their citations. These facts must be taken into consideration if citation data are to be used correctly in evaluating research.

There are times when a researcher would not seek or cannot get clearance to have a piece of research published. Someone doing research on computer or national security may face such a dilemma. Or it is conceivable that a pharmaceutical company may impose an information quarantine and prohibit publishing the results of research carried out under its sponsorship for fear of alerting the competition. One must be sensitive to these possibilities.

Research activity runs the gamut from thinking out an idea and carrying through with the work, to disseminating the results found, to raising the money to allow the work to proceed, to contributing to keep the discipline viable and growing. Research and its practice is discipline-specific; it differs for the humanities professor and the science professor. Recognizing these cultural differences allows us to better appreciate the factors that must be considered when analyzing and understanding what a researcher in English does and why and how his or her methods are different from the scientist. It behooves the evaluator to apply different evaluation measures or expect quantitative variations from discipline to discipline.

When to Evaluate Research

The most common reason for evaluation is to affect behavior. It allows the evaluator to send the right signals and, if the evaluator is an administrator or supervisor, to provide incentives for the researcher to attain established targets. The researcher may need validation by others. The exercise can be conducted once for a single piece of work or annually for raises or for distribution of resources such as travel funds, students, and release time. It can be episodic as when used for grants, awards, promotion, or tenure. The kind of evaluation sought is an important factor in deciding the specifics of the process. There is also an incidental benefit of evaluation: the reason to hire and fire.

How to Evaluate Performance Measures

For a single piece of work and for an evaluator expert in the area, assessment is a no-brainer. Is the idea well thought out? Indeed, is it a well-known, unsolved problem? Is the methodology sound and the execution free from flaws? The answers tell the story. If you are a nonexpert, you check where it is published, you ask if it received a best paper award, you seek the reaction of others from citation counts (the buzz numbers), you check if it has made the conference circuit (as a topic for a panel discussion or even as the reason for the conference itself), you note if the author(s) is(are) being frequently invited to present seminars or colloquia and, if you have the time, you read stalwarts of the popular press to see if responsible media have gotten wind of it. You are relying on the word of others whom you respect.

When the evaluation is episodic and the work of the researcher has to be folded over a period of time, it is appropriate to tally up in aggregate what one is able to do for a single piece of work and then add on a few other measures. Our discussion of the practice of research and the importance of various factors in its execution allows us now to construct a set of quantitative performance indicators for research that may be appropriate when a researcher is up for tenure or promotion. (Most colleges and universities appear to have variations of it.)

- Publication as a senior author at an appropriate rate in refereed scholarly or creative journals or creative work (including musical compositions, art and films, computer codes, computer simulations, electronic teaching material) presented at appropriate venues
- Authorship of scholarly/creative books or monographs or of invited review articles or chapters in books
- Leadership of a program with a good track record of continued extramural funding
- National and international recognition for original contributions through honorific awards such as fellow of a professional society, National Young Investigator, Franklin Medal, Pulitzer Prize
- Editorial appointments to professional journals, reviewer for manuscripts for publication
- Active involvement in professional societies and recognition through election to office
- Favorably reviewed grant proposals
- Invited talks, lectures, readings, performance, or exhibits
- Appointment to advisory committees, review committees of extramural funding agencies, accreditation teams for site visits, consultantships
- Citations that attest to the external professional reputation of the researcher by other scholars in the field (through the volume, as recorded by citation indexing services such as Science Citation Index and CiteSeer)

- Convener/organizer of international conferences or symposia, chair of a session, discussant on a panel
- Service as an external examiner for Ph.D. dissertation defense in another institution
- Peer mentoring, supervision of Ph.D. students
- The time to completion of Ph.D. students and their placement
- Tenure at another institution

Can a scorecard of these indicators be created with simple instructions to fill the spaces? Can a grading system be developed based on evidence gleaned from this typical checklist, one that will stand the tightest scrutiny? Would that suggest that there is a bibliometric way to evaluate? As with many things, the answer is a qualified yes. The devil is in the details. For example, when evaluating the worth of the researcher's publications should we not rate the journals he or she has chosen to publish in as well? What are their standards, their rejection rates, their readerships, and the compositions of their editorial boards? Are there papers in the curriculum vitae that would not have seen the light of day if submitted to top-tier journals? Should the possibility be looked into that the researcher has two or more articles in print that are based on a single research finding, a result of "salami science"? Have multi-authored papers been properly accounted for? Was the researcher the leader in collaborative work or just a useful member of the pack? Do the journals publish in English, the lingua franca of almost all research?

If colleges and universities use citation counts when making decisions about appointments, promotion, and tenure, because these reflect impact, should they not realize that there are ways to game the system? How watchful are we of self-citations? Can we be certain that there is no illegitimate use of coauthorships, friends helping each other out and bumping up the citation rate? If we count seminars and colloquia, how sure are we that there is not an

Old Boys Club at work? You rub my back, I will rub yours. Invite me, and I'll invite you.

External funds in general signal peer approval. Insofar as they allow for the recruitment of research fellows, research faculty, and graduate students who produce more research and more research proposals and hence compete more effectively for funds, the amount of dollars received serves as a rough approximation of the aggregate quality of the researcher's enterprise. This is the measure used almost universally on a national scale to evaluate the research productivity of institutions and for the individual researcher in clinical medicine. It is common practice to take National Institutes of Health funding, secured in open competition, as an absolute measure of the researcher's productivity. But there are funds and then there are funds. Some researchers receive money through pork barrel projects authorized in congressional bills that result from lobbying and influence. Some researchers draw significant support from industry. It is often assumed that industry-sponsored research carries the risk of bias. Is the research influenced? For example, are medical researchers, who receive substantial support from the pharmaceutical industry, held hostage by the companies that have a stake in their findings? Do business interests drive their research agendas? Can it be stated that the research is tainted from collaboration with industry? As opposed to government (not congressional) funds in the U.S., industry hands out money without open competition and peer review. Are these kinds of funds and the research they support then worth less? Because applied research has the connotation of money and the professoriate is by and large money-averse for themselves, it is fair to say that researchers tend to value basic research more: One is not selling out to commercial interests. In general, whenever research smacks of direct financial gain for its proponent or its funding occurs as an earmarked item in a congressional bill, it is less respected.

Because of this need to correctly interpret and understand the real meaning behind the quantitative data when evaluating, the straightforward bibliometric approach must be supplemented by something else. In the past, research evaluation tended to rely on peer review (getting an expert to be the consultant assessor who gives an opinion) since the bibliometric method was thought to be totally unreliable (before the advent of Science Citation Index and PubMed, a directory service, for example). But it is now generally recognized that peer reviews (without any foundation on quantitative data) also have various limitations and shortcomings. Subjectivity is a major problem of peer reviews. The opinions of experts may be influenced by subjective elements, narrow-mindedness, and limited cognitive horizons. What is a nonexpert evaluator to do? It would appear that an argument can be made to use citation indicators and other bibliometric indicators to counteract shortcomings and mistakes in the peers' judgments and to use peer review to return the favor to overcome the deficiencies in the bibliometric method. We need a proper marriage of the two schemes predicated on the principle that the greater the variety of measures and qualitative processes used to evaluate research, the greater the likelihood that a composite measure offers a reliable understanding of the knowledge produced.

On that premise we could include this qualitative indicator in the evaluation:

- Testimonials from experts in the field both inside and outside the institution that the researcher has made original and substantive contributions to the field of research, scholarship, or creative specialty

Whatever data has been collected on the quantitative measures should be shared with the experts, culled from a directory set up with the assistance of citation research. To avoid bias, these authorities should not be coauthors, former major professors or Ph.D. dissertation committee members, or former students. Instructions to the referees would include the following:

> Assess the scholarly contributions in terms of 1) quality and quantity of research compared to other individuals in the same discipline at a similar career stage in general and at your institution; 2) the quality of the journals in which the research has been published; 3) the current and potential contribution of the body of research to the literature; 4) the nature of the research problems selected; and 5) the innovativeness of the approaches used. Referees must also be asked for their curricula vitae so as to establish their credentials for the benefit of reviewers who are not in the field.

Guidelines for Evaluating Research

Even with the performance indicators identified and their purpose understood, it is the small details that matter in the end. As such, the following are some specific suggestions that I believe will be useful when one needs to evaluate faculty research in general or for special cases.

- *Recognize the purpose of the evaluation.* The relative weights of bibliometric measures and peer reviews will depend upon it. Is it to consider a lifetime of work or a single paper? Is it for an award or tenure or promotion or raise? Is it for an individual or a unit or a school? Who will be reading the evaluation?

- *Do not just count the number of pages, or the number of papers, or the total amount of extramural funds, or the number of patents or Ph.D.s mentored.* Remember that researchers, just like other humans, can game any system. Never take things at face value. It is impact that is all-important.

- *Read between the lines of a reference letter. Look at the names that the researcher is being compared to.* Keep in mind whether the letter can be read by the reviewee. If so, there can be a different tone to it. Look for sentences such as "want to recruit so-and-so myself!" and "should receive tenure if at my institution" or conversely " . . . but probably not at mine."

- *Recognize the discipline.* It is important that the evaluator think in discipline-specific ways to give full consideration to the evaluation.

- *Recognize the environment in which the research is being conducted.* It has been found that researchers who belong to units with a critical mass of faculty do produce more and are rewarded more. Does the researcher have extended periods of "quiet" to do his or her work?

- *Look at all indicators.* Check for consistency across the board.

- *Recognize lifecycle factors.* There are peaks and valleys in every researcher's work. A sudden commitment to teaching could take the person away from research. How do you assess a Nobel laureate who no longer publishes?

- *Note that creative research more and more is occurring at the junction between traditional disciplines.* For those who work in an interdisciplinary area their intellectual contributions are difficult to classify. Often they are unfairly held to the standards of a specific discipline. It may be necessary to find or develop an appropriate blend of criteria that must be made available to the researcher as early as possible. Additionally, proper arrangements must be made among the home department and all others. Senior faculty (both internal and external) experienced in such work and familiar with the vicissitudes of working in domains that straddle more than one discipline should be brought into the evaluation process.

Conclusion

Those of us who have to evaluate research want measures of quality and productivity that will not fail us. Bibliometric indicators have a place in the process but so does peer review.

ACKNOWLEDGMENTS

Donna Murasko and Ali Houshmand of Drexel University gave generously of their time to submit to interviews on what they themselves do when called upon to evaluate the quality and productivity of research of faculty members.

SUGGESTED READINGS

The following are useful sources on evaluating research. I recommend them to the reader interested in delving further into this topic.

Bender, E., & Gray, D. (1999, April). The scholarship of teaching. *Research & Creative Activity, 22*(1). Retrieved January 23, 2006, from http://www.indiana.edu/~rcapub/v22n1/p03.html

The collected works of Eugene Garfield: http://www.garfield .library.upenn.edu/

Merrill Advanced Studies Center. (2001, June). *Evaluating research productivity* (University of Kansas Report No. 105). Lawrence, KS: Author.

Research Evaluation, a peer-reviewed, international journal, published every April, August, and December by Beech Tree Publishing. Edited by Anthony van Raan (University of Leiden, The Netherlands) and Susan Cozzens (Georgia Institute of Technology, USA).

Scientometrics, an international journal for all quantitative aspects of the science of science, communication in science, and science policy. Editor-in-chief, T. Braun.

REFERENCES

Boyer, E. L. (1990). *Scholarship reconsidered: Priorities of the professoriate*. Princeton, NJ: Carnegie Foundation for the Advancement of Teaching.

Byrne, J. A. (1990, October 29). Is research in the ivory tower "fuzzy, irrelevant, pretentious"? *BusinessWeek*, 62–66.

Garfield, E. (1980). Is information retrieval in the arts and humanities inherently different from that in science? The effect that ISI®'s citation index for the arts and humanities is expected to have on future scholarship. *Library Quarterly, 50*(1), 40–57.

Rice, R. E. (1996). *Making a place for the new American scholar* (New Pathways Project Inquiry No. 1). Washington, DC: American Association for Higher Education.

Shulman, L. S. (2000, April). From Minsk to Pinsk: Why a scholarship of teaching and learning? *Journal of the Scholarship of Teaching and Learning, 1*(1), 48–52.

Teaching Evaluation Follies: Misperception and Misbehavior in Student Evaluations of Teachers

10

Jane S. Halonen, George B. Ellenberg

> *The first principle is that you must not fool yourself—and you are the easiest person to fool.*
>
> —Richard Phillips Feynman

The specifics may vary from campus to campus, but the basic ritual unfolds each semester in a similar fashion in a majority of our classes. At some point close to the end of the course, the professor transports an official envelope filled with Likert-based rating forms that have ample space for narrative descriptions and, of course, Number 2 pencils (see Chapter 4). The professor appoints a trusted student to govern the distribution and collection of the forms and then leaves class early so students can write their feedback in an unfettered fashion. Long after the course is over, the tabulated results come back to the instructor and the instructor's supervisor. Usually handwritten feedback has been laboriously typed to protect student identity. Whether the results get careful review or merely find their way to the circular file, campuses invest countless hours and massive resources in this process as part of the shift to accountability in higher education.

Evaluating the quality of teaching in higher education is tricky business, but it is now a familiar component of the higher education landscape. In fact, researchers have produced more than 2,000 studies on the many aspects of student evaluation of instruction (Centra, 2003). Performed partly because of outside mandates, most often at the state level, assessing teaching makes sense because it can lead to improved teaching. Yet practically no campus is satisfied with the protocols it has in place for evaluating teaching. The quest for perfecting the teaching evaluation process is quite likely doomed to be unending as we fuss and fiddle with terminology, question wording, and compare strategies. But it is in the fussing and fiddling that we move toward a better understanding of what goes on in the college and university classroom.

Many students dutifully complete faculty evaluation forms and provide heartfelt, and sometimes heartwarming, feedback to the faculty who have made them treasure their time in the classroom. We have seen students who describe heroic efforts by their instructors that have turned the students' lives around or have inspired them to greater achievements. For example, a student writes that the professor "has opened my eyes in her teaching ability and inspired me to reach for what I want and who I want to become." Time with a truly talented teacher *can* make a profound difference, and such potent relationships are regularly part of the teaching evaluation landscape. On the other end of the evaluation spectrum are those cases that reflect how painful classes can be due to poor faculty planning and implementation as well as disregard for student learning. Most faculty, of course, fall between these extremes, and most faculty are "good teachers." McKeachie (2005) appropriately suggests that faculty who strive for continuous improvement will have no need to worry about the larger issue of personnel evaluation, which provides reassurance that student evaluations can play a role in continuous improvement if the process unfolds properly.

The issue we wish to address in this chapter is how student evaluations fit into the larger portrait of a faculty member's teaching persona as well as how best to carry out the teaching evaluation process. Unfortunately, we contend that there is a great deal of foolishness on the part of all the key players who participate in teaching evaluations: students, faculty, and administrators. Our purpose in this chapter is to shed some light on our collective foolishness and suggest some alternatives to improve the process.

Student Follies

No matter where the faculty member falls on the continuum of exceptional to unacceptable teaching, students often derail the effectiveness of the evaluation process by committing an assortment of foolish gestures. What kinds of follies do students commit, thereby diminishing our ability to make sense of the process?

- *They fade.* Even when students provide favorable numerical ratings, they may not be inclined to write much that provides the instructor with concrete ideas about what aspects of performance led to the high ratings.

- *They suck up.* Sometimes praise is so thick that the quality feels a bit surreal. It is not always easy to identify sincere, positive feedback from the syrupy, manipulative kind. Nor is it understandable why students might invest time in such activity when it will not have a direct relationship to their grades.

- *They go woebegone.* Despite our cherished objective of improving students' critical thinking skills, there are students with such a profound positive evaluation bias (i.e., everyone is above average) that they would be unable to bestow negative ratings on anyone. Therefore, even the very worst teachers may be able to take refuge in the generous responses of such students.

- *They go blue.* An unpleasant reality in postmodern times is that students feel little restraint with regard to profanity. Teachers "suck." Students "feel screwed." And it only goes downhill from here.

- *They go for the jugular.* Students can sometimes be very mean-spirited in their commentary. For example, students have been known to attack an instructor's heritage, breeding, intelligence, sense of humor (or lack of it), and income to try to inflict psychological pain as revenge for their perceptions that the class disappointed them.

- *They mob.* Sometimes students coordinate their harsh feedback in the hopes that a unified front can prompt corrective action. They demand firing, drawing, quartering, or publicly burning at the stake.

- *They calculate their losses.* When unhappy, students will make references to the exact financial losses that have accrued to their wasted time in the classroom.

- *They lose focus.* How many professors have had to endure comments about their hair, fashion style, or other irrelevant personal characteristics rather than getting information that could be useful in improving the course?

- *They use alien and imprecise language.* Scaling to the top of student regard is likely to generate a variety of standard "hip" praise, including the overused "awesome," "coolest," and "He rocks!" Although pleasant to hear in some ways, such comments offer little help for someone interested in improvement.

- *They turn seductive.* Some students appear to assume that the teaching feedback is an opportunity to have an intensely personal conversation with the faculty member, which can result in some fairly embarrassing text. A student once gushed about her professor, "He *looks* good, *smells* good, and *feels* good."

- *They delude themselves.* One recent student critic demanded, "Either this professor goes or *I* go!" Students simply do not understand how much or how little power their individual perceptions play in larger decisions.

- *They become agents.* Students who are enamored with an instructor may think the teaching evaluation is the place to advocate for better conditions for their favorite professor. They misunderstand the complexity that influences personnel decisions.

Faculty Follies

No matter how seasoned the faculty member, there is a moment when you open the results and wonder if you still have what it takes to make the classroom work. Many faculty enact the process in good faith, dutifully examine the results to see what kinds of suggestions might emerge to help them improve their work, and fine-tune their courses accordingly. However, professors are also inclined to foolish behavior that impairs their ability to make best use of the results.

- *They "forget."* Some professors just cannot take precious time away from covering the assigned content and relegate evaluation to an activity that is completed only if they are caught up.
- *They taint.* Administering evaluation processes following a particularly challenging test is usually not sound practice. Neither is waiting to hand out evaluations until a particularly troublesome student is absent. Sometimes the instructor may give students but a few minutes to hastily bubble in their evaluations. Such actions lead to questionable validity.
- *They pander.* Some professors have well-developed reputations for "coincidentally" bringing treats for the class session in which they plan to conduct the evaluation.
- *They wheedle.* Students report that some faculty openly discuss the impact of negative reviews and even suggest that the care and feeding of their families may depend on students offering favorable feedback. Other faculty mention that they do not yet have tenure in the context of discussing the importance of teaching evaluations.
- *They script.* Sometimes numerous evaluations in one class are so similar that it is obvious the faculty member primed students with topics to address in the evaluations. This may be an honest attempt to motivate students to add written comments, but it

indicates a level of input that the instructor should not have in the process.

- *They barter.* Some faculty may exchange strong evaluations from students for easy grading standards. Everyone looks good as a result, but there may be little learning going on in the process.

- *They linger.* A few professors get dinged appropriately by complaining students because they do not leave the room during the evaluation period, making it hard for students to engage in the process candidly. In some settings, this may merely corrupt the evaluation process; in other settings it may violate university or state rules. The worst-case scenario, of course, is when the instructor not only remains in the classroom, but also takes up the evaluations and has access to them before the institution tabulates the results. Even if the instructor is scrupulously honest about not looking at the evaluations outside of established channels, the process is tainted.

- *They overrespond.* It is surprisingly easy even for very experienced faculty to become preoccupied with the nasty minority rather than taking comfort from the typical majority of really good reviews. By the same token, professors may be inclined to attribute too much power or truth to the positive reviews they receive.

- *They denigrate.* Faculty often take refuge in an assortment of defenses against the validity of negative evaluations. They argue that class size, course level, time of day, gender, professor seasoning, and discipline, among other variables, all exert undue influence on the outcome of student teaching evaluations. Ory (2001) suggests there is compelling data that elective courses tend to be rated more highly than required courses, but that is the only variable that exerts consistent and strong influence on student ratings. Similarly, Arreola (1995) describes the relationship between grades and evaluations as "the single-most frequently researched issue" (p. 85), but concludes that support for this correlation is decidedly weak.

- *They ignore.* A particular problem for teaching veterans, some faculty simply trash the results without examining them carefully for whatever lessons might be conveyed—positive and negative. Even the most experienced instructor may glean important insights from a careful reading of student evaluations. Indeed, struggling students may be the very best critics about the changes that would help render a class more effective.

Administrative Follies

The administrators who set the faculty evaluation process in motion represent the third category of characters who misperceive and/or misbehave. Most administrators try to be evenhanded in the manner in which they interpret teaching evaluation data. They institute procedures that protect confidentiality for the students and respect privacy for the faculty. However, they, too, engage in actions that may detract from the validity and value of the evaluations.

- *They neglect.* Administrators may expect that the evaluation process can be conducted validly and reliably without any specific training or oversight. Relying on pure common sense of all concerned to ensure valid and reliable results is a bad idea.
- *They constrain.* If there is one point to be stressed about the evaluation process, it is the importance of not relying on a single index for evaluating teaching (Centra, 1993; Seldin & Associates, 1999). Administrators should not ignore other obvious avenues of feedback about teaching quality (e.g., syllabus design, exam construction, assessment strategies, peer reviews, videotaped performances, etc.) if they are serious about helping faculty improve.
- *They conflate.* An evaluative item that regularly shows up on student evaluation forms is something like "Instructor shows mastery of information." Just how would a student be in a position to

make such a judgment? Teaching evaluation formats should be constructed from the point of view of what the student is competent to analyze.

- *They obfuscate.* Every campus struggles with getting just the right language for making fine discriminations. But how is a student to know the difference between someone who is *outstanding* versus *excellent* versus *distinguished*?

- *They jeopardize.* Not engaging in appropriate procedures to ensure confidentiality could facilitate faculty retribution in future courses and will certainly justify students' unwillingness to provide developmental feedback to faculty.

- *They delay.* By returning information to faculty members well after the course is over, whatever opportunity the professor had to correct problems legitimately for the current crop of complainants is gone (see Chapter 11).

- *They quantify.* Some administrators accept student evaluation data as conclusive evidence of teaching quality in the absence of other data sources. Usually narrative material is heartfelt and may provide solid feedback about what faculty members could do to change. However, numbers are crisper and easier to manipulate statistically. In worst-case scenarios, the numbers may be used to establish extremely competitive rankings of quality within a department, and the numbers alone may dictate the size of a merit raise.

- *They assume.* Many administrators believe that high ratings probably mean the professor is giving grades away or, conversely, that low ratings signify the professor is valiantly holding the line against grade inflation. That relationship is an easy one to verify. Some of the most challenging professors with normal distributions—as many Fs as As—will end up with strong evaluations because students can tell the difference between a professor with standards and one without.

- *They succumb.* Although students may equate "Fun class and funny guy" with substantive learning, this may not always be the case, especially if the student employs the passive voice, as in "I was kept entertained." Students are often very generous with praise for faculty members who tell good stories but whose narratives tend to focus on minutiae that may be relatively unimportant for their long-term learning. Administrators should vigilantly ensure that faculty exercise appropriate rigor if the degree to be conferred is worth the tuition.

- *They shirk.* This failure is most obvious at the administrative level when the chair has not actually observed the instructor in the classroom. Thus there is no link between what students say and what the reviewer genuinely knows to be the case. This situation is especially problematic during a faculty member's pre-tenure years.

- *They normalize.* Some administrators expect that faculty evaluations in their realm of responsibility should generate a normal distribution, with a few faculty in the distinguished category to balance the few who need remediation while the majority of faculty represent the "average" level of achievement. The problem with this expectation is that years of education have winnowed the faculty to a highly select and well-prepared group of professionals. It simply does not make sense to expect such high achievers to fit the normal curve.

- *They stop short.* Ory (2000) points out that few campuses have recommended protocols in place that can help faculty make sense of poor ratings and develop specific strategies for improvement. For the most part, once a faculty member receives negative news, that person may be left to stew. Such a disruption in the corrective cycle puts undue emphasis on the ratings for personnel decisions rather than facilitating true teaching reform.

A Better Way

Although considerable foolishness is possible from all players, there are several recommendations that could enhance the value of this standard practice. We offer a baker's dozen of concrete suggestions for improving the process, recognizing that there is unlikely to be a one-size-fits-all protocol to address the many challenges we have outlined.

1) Enhance the Climate

Narrow the window in which you gather evaluations to a standard, short timeframe, with a promotional campaign that supports the importance of the process. The campaign could include posters and email reminders to faculty and students to highlight the significance of the time investment.

2) Automate

Explore moving the entire process to an online procedure that can be completed without disrupting class time. This approach would substantially reduce many of the temptations faculty experience when they must accommodate evaluation activities in an already overfull course plan. Although we can hear registrars across the country screaming at this suggestion, it may be possible to require students to complete an evaluation before grades are released.

3) Expand Data Sources

For campuses serious about high-quality teaching, other avenues of evaluation need to be considered and incorporated. Systematic peer visits offer an excellent opportunity to verify teaching quality and initiate support systems that many beginning instructors so badly need (see Chapter 6). Scrutiny of syllabi, exams, and assignment design can provide more insights into how the instructor thinks about education. Encouraging the development and updating of a teaching portfolio will provide the best context for understanding how all the datasets fit together in the evolution of the teaching professional.

4) Provide Training . . .

Institute a new faculty orientation session to explain the philosophy and mechanics of the campus evaluation system. A good session should also include pointers on how to prepare for and cope with unpleasant evaluations.

5) . . . and Retraining

Department chairs can offer brief retraining opportunities during regular meetings every two or three years to provide reasonable coverage for faculty members at all levels of career development.

6) Require Reflection and Goal-Setting

Faculty members will be more likely to use constructive feedback for course improvement if they are asked to make sense of what they learn from their students and to set improvement goals that reflect reasonable suggestions. The annual review process may need retooling to give faculty members an opportunity to tell their stories, make sense of their professional adventures, and incorporate new strategies to address improvement. Asking faculty to take evaluations seriously can contribute to keeping their teaching fresh and vital over time.

7) Clarify Format

Standardize the evaluative anchors used on the Likert scale across the campus to facilitate equitable review practices. Asking students to make fine distinctions between *excellent, outstanding,* and *distinctive* will be frustrating in the absence of operational definitions of what those terms convey. Whatever labels are used, a simple explanation that helps students apply the scale to their learning situations will be more effective. A simpler rating scale, adapted from McKeachie (personal communication, January 3, 2005), might suggest just three overall options:

- The instructor was exemplary → give the instructor a raise!
- The instructor was competent → give the instructor my compliments and thanks.
- The instructor was substandard → work with the instructor to develop a remediation plan.

In addition, the open-ended nature of narrative feedback would be fine-tuned by providing a focus question—What can this instructor do to improve the course experience for future students?

8) Respect the Limits of Expertise

Do not ask students to judge whether faculty are experts. They can assess enthusiasm, organization, compassion, accessibility, and other dimensions of teaching, but not disciplinary expertise. Think about what students should legitimately and expertly be in position to address constructively and design the form from that point of view.

9) Encourage Midpoint Feedback Processes

Formal teaching evaluations transpire at the conclusion of a course when students cannot benefit from changes. Instructors and their immediate students can benefit from gathering feedback as they go. One-minute assessment practices (Angelo & Cross, 1993) can provide formative feedback. McKeachie (2005) also recommends an informal teaching evaluation before the end of the semester. Asking students, "What am I doing that is assisting your learning?" and "What could I do that would help you learn more effectively?" conveys your concern to the students. We think gathering those data and taking action to address any problems that arise virtually guarantees higher ratings when the formal procedures take place.

9) Interpret Results Wisely

Administrators should never accept student evaluation numbers at face value. How do the numbers look across courses? What do they suggest about relative strengths and weaknesses in working with different courses? How do these numbers contrast with patterns of grade distributions? Is there an overall trend in the numbers improving or declining? All of these can be elements of a helpful faculty development conversation.

10) Contextualize

Good administrators should take time to put teaching evaluations in context with their faculty members. Although research (e.g., Ory, 2001) suggests that only elective versus required status regularly correlates with teaching evaluation, any specific evaluation could be influenced by class size, time of day, and complexity of demand, all of which can make a difference in the consequences that might follow. If the evaluative results are very bad, setting context is even more important. Simply taking time to explain that adverse patterns may happen even to the best teachers can build the administrator-faculty relationship (see Chapter 3).

11) Address Response Bias

New faculty especially need to understand routine patterns of response bias in student evaluations. For example, every class is likely to have nay-sayers and yay-sayers whose responses reflect more of their own personalities than specifics from the class or the instructors. It may be useful to encourage faculty members to psychologically lop off the extreme 5% of either end of the evaluative curve to address that problem. It is important that faculty not wallow in the unhappiness of the disenfranchised few or take too much credit from the too-generous feedback provided by uncritical students.

12) Abandon Normalizing

We should expect excellence as our classroom standard. Performance that does not meet a standard of excellence is likely to render a faculty member's quest for tenure and promotion a much more hazardous process. Our faculty development strategies need to provide good models with specific criteria about the kinds of behaviors that constitute excellence. Asking departments to generate exemplars that communicate more clearly finer performance discriminations will provide necessary guidance for annual evaluation processes and career planning. Adopting criterion-based evaluation strategies will be far more satisfying and constructive than relying on an instructor's relative position in a normal distribution of student evaluation ratings.

13) Raise the Bar

Perhaps the most important reform we wish to suggest involves taking specific steps to help students develop a better understanding of the role this process should play in improving the quality of the academic experience. We have drafted the following paragraph as a possible standard for in-class teaching evaluation practices. Although it may add a minute or two to the process, communicating these expectations to students should produce a more serious effort that will give faculty focused feedback for their improvement efforts.

> This course evaluation is an important means for you to express your view of your classroom experience. Although we assess the quality of instruction in many ways on this campus, we place great value on student input because of the unique perspective you have on what occurs in the classroom throughout the semester. Thus you are important partners in the process of making the course more effective, the instructor more attuned to his or her strengths and weaknesses, and the university a better place to learn. As such, we ask you to treat the process professionally, seriously, sensitively, and collegially. Consider the questions carefully and answer truthfully. Offer substantive written comments when you deem them appropriate since you may offer insights that standard questions miss. As members of the higher education community and participants in the learning

process, you have both the privilege and the responsibility to take the evaluation process seriously. Importantly, instructors will not have access to course evaluations until after grades have been posted. We will treat the evaluation forms as the confidential documents that they are. These general guidelines also should be followed:

- You should be given a minimum of 15 minutes to complete the evaluation.
- The instructor should not be present when you are completing the evaluation.
- The designated representative should deliver the results promptly to the proper office.

Student evaluations of teaching are a fact of life. With careful consideration, thoughtful design, and implementation with integrity, they offer a critical piece of information that can help faculty and administrators alike in the evolution of a learning-centered campus.

REFERENCES

Angelo, T. A., & Cross, K. P. (1993). *Classroom assessment techniques: A handbook for college teachers* (2nd ed.). San Francisco, CA: Jossey-Bass.

Arreola, R. A. (1995). *Developing a comprehensive faculty evaluation system: A handbook for college faculty and administrators on designing and operating a comprehensive faculty evaluation system.* Bolton, MA: Anker.

Centra, J. A. (1993). *Reflective faculty evaluation: Enhancing teaching and determining faculty effectiveness.* San Francisco, CA: Jossey-Bass.

Centra, J. A. (2003). Will teachers receive higher student evaluations by giving higher grades and less course work? *Research in Higher Education, 44*(5), 495–518.

McKeachie, W. J. (2005). *Teaching tips: Strategies, research, and theory for college and university teachers* (12th ed.). Boston, MA: Houghton Mifflin.

Ory, J. C. (2000). Teaching evaluation: Past, present, and future. In K. E. Ryan (Ed.), *New directions for teaching and learning: No. 83. Evaluating teaching in higher education: A vision for the future* (pp. 13–18). San Francisco, CA: Jossey-Bass.

Ory, J. (2001). Faculty thoughts and concerns about student ratings. In K. G. Lewis (Ed.), *New directions for teaching and learning: No. 87. Techniques and strategies for interpreting student evaluations* (pp. 3–15). San Francisco, CA: Jossey-Bass.

Seldin, P., & Associates. (1999). *Changing practices in evaluating teaching: A practical guide to improved faculty performance and promotion/tenure decisions.* Bolton, MA: Anker.

Using Evaluation Data to Improve Teaching Effectiveness

11

Todd Zakrajsek

"I just don't know what to do." As the director of a faculty center for teaching and learning I frequently hear statements such as this. Faculty are often frustrated when trying to create effective learning environments for their students. It would be absurd to expect our students to grow and change as learned individuals without feedback with respect to their work. Changes to improve their performance based on that feedback is also expected. Finding effective methods to approach a problem, deciding what types of data to collect, discovering ways to convey the solution to others, and obtaining appropriate feedback are all necessary steps for students to become educated individuals. Why should the process be any different for developing effective teachers?

Teaching demands continual growth, and there are many sources of data to consider when improving teaching performance: Self-evaluation, student ratings, peer evaluation, and classroom assessment techniques are just a few. The difficulty lies in gathering appropriate data and then using the data to effectively change the way we approach the classroom experience. Research indicates that consultation or assistance with interpreting data such as student ratings is almost a necessary component of improving teaching and learning (Seldin & Associates, 1999).

Initial Considerations

In considering how to use evaluation data to improve performance it is important to be mindful of the instructor's place within the academy. Advice is often very different for seasoned professors than for new faculty, for tenured faculty versus untenured faculty. For some individuals, the pros and cons of making adjustments in one's teaching need to be considered. Often, it is a consideration of academic politics. This is a sensitive point for many, as it would seem unethical to withhold a potentially ideal learning environment for fear of reprisal from one's colleagues. That said, if a department primarily consists of full professors who lecture all the time, it might place a new faculty member in harm's way with respect to promotion and tenure to suggest he or she move to a largely collaborative classroom structure.

Higher education is a somewhat closed system. To be successful with pedagogical change, we must be mindful of the environment in which we work. Department politics aside, change is often good, and student learning may be greatly enhanced by using evaluation data to improve teaching performance.

Self-Evaluation

Getting Started

When a faculty member wishes to improve his or her teaching effectiveness, I first request a statement of teaching philosophy and a self-evaluation. The teaching philosophy is a short reflective essay outlining one's beliefs about student learning and the best pedagogical approaches, including specific actions, to facilitate that learning. Ideally, a teaching philosophy includes teaching goals for the instructor, learning goals for the students, and desired areas to improve the interaction. Once the teaching philosophy statement is finalized, the faculty member completes a self-assessment to document the extent to which expectations are being realized. Self-assessment is helpful for any teacher, but it is particularly useful for those eager to change and those who are fully willing to take responsibility for their own behavior and how that behavior impacts student learning.

Using Self-Assessment

Once the teaching philosophy and self-assessment is completed, the realism of the statement must be considered. A faculty center for teaching and learning can help with this task. If no such center exists, one can ask a friend or colleague to read the statement and respond. In the worst-case scenario, faculty can critically evaluate their own self-assessment by looking for areas that are very important and yet deficient in their current teaching. It is important to not be too hard on oneself. We *all* need to work on our teaching. Many individuals focus on what is not working well and fail to mention the positive aspects. There is a good possibility that the faculty member is stronger than he or she thinks. Make sure to celebrate what is done well and include that along with the noted deficiencies.

The faculty member should read carefully what he or she hopes to accomplish in the classroom and behaviors that can be engaged to work toward that goal. These behaviors are extremely important and should be as objective as possible. Consider the following example in which Chris, frustrated by inconsistency noted after completing a self-evaluation, outlines specific behaviors to improve performance.

Chris feels students should receive prompt feedback, yet it seems to take a long time to return term papers. By developing an objective statement of future behaviors, Chris will know when teaching behavior is improving. In this case, Chris decides that all written papers are to be returned within two class periods of when they are received. To accomplish this goal, two considerations are needed: the types of assignments given and when the papers are due. Chris teaches a Monday/Wednesday class and tends to procrastinate on tasks such as grading, so it would be better to have papers due on a Monday rather than a Wednesday. In this situation, two class periods following a Monday due date will be the following Monday. If Chris does not begin grading until a day or two before the papers are to be returned to students, the entire weekend is available for grading.

Cautions Regarding Self-Assessment

A specific challenge with respect to self-assessment is that it can be influenced by one's mood (Atwater, 1998). It is often good to review self-assessment a few times over the course of a week after it has been written. Self-assessment is problematical for those who are unable to reflect on their own behavior. Raters who find self-criticism difficult often blame others for their poor performance (Braskamp & Ory, 1994; Wilson & Pearson, 1995). If a faculty member finds it hard to accept that what he or she does as the instructor is a predominant factor in student learning, self-assessment will be particularly troublesome.

Validating Self-Evaluation

One method to determine if the instructor is meeting his or her goals is to obtain student data. Student end-of-course ratings and classroom feedback acquired during the semester can be very helpful. For example, if the instructor indicates in a self-assessment that he or she demonstrates respect in the classroom, the instructor can note the extent to which students agree with the student rating item, "The instructor treated students in this course with respect." It is important to remember that this information can and should be used in conjunction with self-evaluations.

Student Ratings

Getting Started

Information from student ratings of instruction contain students' opinions or perceptions of teaching. These often reflect reality, but not always. When using these data to improve performance, keep in mind that it may simply be the opinions or perceptions that need to be addressed, not the specific behavior itself. For example, if students report that the instructor is not accessible, then that is their perception. It may be that the instructor really is not in his office very often. It might also be that the instructor is perceived to be inaccessible. One cannot simply respond, "I am in my office 90 hours per week. How can they say I am not accessible?" In working with faculty I always ask individuals to reframe such a response to, "If you are in your office 90 hours per week, why do you think your students feel you are inaccessible?"

In one case, after much discussion and several class visits, I noted the instructor constantly talked to me about how busy she was and that she had to work almost 100 hours per week to keep up with all she needed to do. In asking one of her students about the availability of the instructor the student responded, "I would never dream of bothering her in her office, she is always so busy." That instructor was perceived as being inaccessible due to a wall she had inadvertently constructed between herself and her students. In this case it was not actual availability, but rather the image she projected to her students that needed to be changed.

In addition to perceptions, student ratings are a valuable resource for learning about what works and what needs attention in the classroom. No individual will observe more of a faculty member's teaching than students, putting them in an ideal role to offer input.

End-of-Course Ratings

End-of-course evaluations typically are made up of forced-response items and open-ended items. When I begin to work with faculty I first look at the closed-ended questions. These are the items that ask students to indicate to what extent they agree with a statement (e.g., "The instructor seemed well prepared for class.") or the extent to which a faculty member engages in a specific behavior (e.g., "How frequently does the instructor arrive to class on time?"). Faculty should not look at the numbers with excessive specificity. When using student ratings to enhance one's teaching effectiveness, look for general trends. The difference between 3.00 and 2.95 on a 4-point scale should be ignored, but the difference between 1.03 and 3.45 is very much of interest.

Ideally, an instructor should note student input from multiple classes and across several semesters. Classes often take on personalities of their own. It is not uncommon to have two identical courses in a given semester in which ratings are higher in one course than another. Also, focus on classes with relatively large numbers and those where most of the students have completed the survey. If one has less than 10 students in a class, ignore means and look at the distribution of the scores. With small classes, a single low score will greatly influence the mean. Likewise, a class where less than one-half of the students have filled out the survey will typically be biased.

Next, look for items of most concern based on one's teaching philosophy. If all areas are lower than desired, do not try to fix everything at once. Instead, select two or three items on which to work at any given time. For example, students may rate the instructor low on "Returning course material in a timely manner." First, ask why students would perceive the faculty member low on an item for which there is concern. Do not focus on the immediate reaction of, "How can they say that?" or "Given the size of the class how do they expect me to return 200 papers quickly?" The point is they did find the instructor lacking in a specific area, and typically there is a reason. At times, one will recognize the reason for the lower scores and can begin to work on the issue immediately the next semester. However, there will not always be obvious reasons for student responses. If the cause for a low rating cannot be identified, it may simply point to a potential issue that requires more data. (See http://www.idea.ksu.edu/podidea/index.html for information on a national project that is developing resources to help instructors determine potential causes for low ratings on a given evaluation item.)

The written comments from student ratings are very useful for improving teaching performance. But they can also be among the most difficult to accept. It is often helpful to ask a friend to assist with this task. There will almost always be off-the-wall comments, but they will not render all of the written feedback from students meaningless. Instead, they simply demonstrate the inability of some individuals to provide helpful feedback. At some point in their teaching career many faculty receive comments such as, "I don't like the way you dress," "You look like my brother—I can't stand my brother," and "You need to be fired, now." Up to 10% of written comments, and comments such as these specifically, should be set aside immediately. They are not helpful in improving teaching performance. The only individual comments that must be considered in all cases are those dealing with racism, sexism, or any other ism. These are serious statements, and all claims of discrimination must be taken into account. Even today there are some college classrooms with few students of color. In a class of 40 students, if there is only one person of color, it could be that single student who writes, "This teacher is racist." It is important to note that such claims are to be *considered*. A teacher is not guilty of racism based on a single student comment, but if there are other issues such comments are worthy of further investigation.

Keeping in mind the 10% rule, one effective approach to students' written comments is to read just the first item response for the entire class. Then consider the following three open-ended items: 1) "What does this instructor do that facilitates learning in this class?" 2) "What does this instructor do that hinders learning in this class?" and 3) "What suggestions do you have for this instructor to increase learning in this class?" Start by reading all of the responses to the first question as quickly as possible, making a new pile for each general category described. If the first student stated, "This instructor is really great. She gives us tons of examples and that really helps me to learn a lot and that is why I like this class," this response would be put in the pile reflecting good examples. A response of, "I like the real-life examples in class, they are really fun," would go in the same pile. Keep making unique piles until the responses are all considered. Again, one will typically end up with a pile of a few odd responses. At the end, look at each pile and consider the number of responses in each. If in a class of 35 evaluations completed there are 15 notations of many examples and 5 responses discussing respect, those are the issues students feel deserve attention.

Do the same thing for the other open-ended items. The strength of this approach is that it decreases the consideration of individual responses and allows one to look at categories.

In using the written responses to improve performance, there are some areas of caution. If only a few students complain about some aspect of a course and there are no positive comments about that item, resist the urge to change that dimension of the course. Early in my career four students in a class of 30 stated they hated the text. No one in the class stated they liked it so I thought the text should be changed. The next semester I changed the text and a colleague asked me why. I related that students had disliked it. I now realize most students were satisfied with the text but focused on more salient issues about the class when writing about what they liked. For those who didn't have much negative to say about the class they felt they needed to write something, so they commented that they did not care for the text. I am now convinced the change of text was totally unnecessary. Had 20 of the 30 students commented they disliked the text it would have been worth talking to students about the text in more detail. The point here is to not let a few squeaky wheels cause a faculty member to change what might be working well in his or her class.

Immediate Feedback Techniques

Instead of waiting until the end of the semester, faculty should ask for feedback on issues related to student learning at least twice during the semester. This is a minimum, and I often suggest to faculty they seek feedback once every two weeks. I am becoming more and more convinced that end-of-course data, with respect to improving performance, should simply serve as an indication of where to focus data collection the following semester. If used properly, immediate feedback generates valuable information and allows one to make small adjustments as the class progresses.

If an institution allows it, one can use the same form for mid-semester feedback that is used at the end of the semester. An alternative is to develop the questions oneself. The feedback I typically request of my students includes the following: "What encourages learning in this class?" and "Is there anything you feel would further encourage learning in this class?"

Asking questions in this way does not directly point to any specific aspect of the course. There is also no request for identifying weaknesses or deficiencies. If any come to mind they can be addressed in the second question, but otherwise I see no reason to prompt for them. It is important to go over the responses before the next class period. Students will write good responses if they know the information is used. Therefore, if issues surface that can be changed, let the students know the next class period that there will be a change. If there is something that cannot be changed, let the students know the next class period why the change cannot be implemented. An example of a response for the next class period might be as follows:

> Thank you for the feedback. Many of you noted I talk too quickly at times. Starting today, if I am talking too quickly, simply put a hand up so I can see. You don't need to wave your hand over your head, just let me see it so I know to slow down. Some have also stated the text is too dry and has too much research. I am sorry about that, but I selected this text specifically because of the research discussed. It is important to be able to read research results.

Students regularly report they appreciate faculty who listen to their concerns and make adjustments when necessary. This method allows for that.

A more structured and formal method used to collect student information on classroom instruction is the small group instructional diagnosis (SGID), which uses facilitated small group discussion among students to provide feedback to an instructor. This approach collects information for teaching improvement, but it also promotes student involvement in the teaching and learning process by developing ideas for strengthening the course and enhancing communication between instructor and students about the teaching and learning process (Clark & Redmond, 1982). It takes training to complete a SGID properly, but the information is very valuable.

Cautions Regarding Student Ratings

In many respects the best information for improving teaching comes directly from students. Who better to say if they are learning than the individuals in the class? However, there are obvious areas of caution. Students may not always know the best strategies for learning and therefore may not know how to advise the instructor to help them learn more effectively.

Students may also focus too much on how well they are doing in the class and not enough on the learning taking place. When returning examinations to students I used to report the mean and grade distribution, often showing individual scores along a curve that approached a normal distribution. Now I spend more time talking about the learning and how students approach issues differently and more effectively at midterm than they did at the beginning of the semester. The reason for the distinction is that students are very sensitive to working diligently in class and receiving grades that appear lower than expected. Feedback received from students regarding teaching effectiveness may be greatly biased in courses where they feel the instructor is "too difficult" if the focus is only on the grades received.

Peer Evaluation Data

Peers are a valuable source of data to improve teaching effectiveness. They can visit classes and provide feedback on the learning environment created. They can also review teaching materials and provide suggestions for improvement on the syllabus, examinations, grading rubrics, extra-credit assignments, and amount of material covered in the course. In some situations, it might be valuable to have a peer meet with the students at the end of a class session to gather additional evaluation data.

Getting Started

If peer evaluations are required, there may be established guidelines for who will conduct the evaluation and perhaps even when it will be done. If such requirements are not in place some decisions will have to be made, one of the most important being who to ask for assistance in gathering information on teaching effectiveness. The evaluator must be someone who is respected, or the information received will be easy to dismiss. He or she must also be trusted to keep the information confidential, be kind, and be willing to give constructive feedback, especially if this is the instructor's first peer evaluation. It will be of no assistance to have someone observe a class only to tell the instructor that everything is fine. The evaluator can also be a colleague from another department, but it is important that a peer outside the instructor's discipline understand at minimum the basics of what is being taught.

There is a difference between peer evaluation for summative and formative use. The goal for formative use is to find anything that might assist one to be a better instructor. Such detail is often not pointed out in summative evaluation. For that reason it is important that formative evaluation data never be used to make personnel decisions.

I often suggest to faculty that they observe a colleague's class before their own class is observed. Following the observation they should discuss with the colleague the major aspects of the course and why the course was taught the way it was. Observing a colleague's course and discussing pedagogical approaches helps an instructor to better understand the value of the process and reduces the anxiety of being observed and evaluated.

Peer Observation of Teaching

Before the class visit the faculty member should provide the evaluator with a copy of his or her teaching philosophy and discuss briefly his or her vision of an ideal class session. This allows a framework for the individual conducting the observation. Next, the specific day the visit will occur and the rubric the observer will use for the evaluation should be selected. Setting an advanced date allows the instructor to plan accordingly so the evaluator can see what he or she is capable of doing in the classroom. A meeting between the instructor and evaluator to discuss the observation should follow the class visit. The observer should then visit the same class unannounced one or two times over the remainder of the semester. The purpose is to receive information from a typical class period. If the observer is able to come to multiple class sessions it is important to specifically address the issues bought up during the previous discussions. This demonstrates that one's teaching has improved and that the feedback was beneficial.

Another approach calls for a colleague to complete a peer observation and then spend approximately the last 10 minutes of the class with the students without the instructor present. The observer gives the students about 5 minutes to write their responses to two questions: "What encourages learning in this class?" and "Is there anything you feel would further encourage learning in this class?" The observer and students then discuss the two questions. If the class has all very positive comments, the observer asks for some suggestions to pass on to the instructor. If the class has primarily negative comments, the observer prompts the group to supply some positive feedback. The student comments are then incorporated into the peer observation. This is much more informative and potentially useful to the instructor since the information has come from a peer and students in the course.

Peer Review of Teaching Materials

In addition to observing the way a class is conducted, it is valuable to ask a colleague to review supportive instructional materials. The best gain will come from a colleague who is familiar with the course and its placement in the department and is able to provide constructive feedback.

The reviewer should first read the teaching philosophy statement, examine the syllabus, and determine the suitability of the text chosen and the amount of content covered in the course. If completed examinations are available, ask the colleague to read through them to see if they are set at the appropriate level. Grading rubrics and other assignments should also be shared, as well as graded essay responses and term papers to see if the instructor's grading is consistent with others in the department (see Chapter 6).

Cautions Regarding Peer Observation and Review of Teaching Materials

Peer review of teaching is perhaps most beneficial to newer members of the department. To have colleagues assist in setting the proper level of rigor in the class and providing helpful tips on pedagogical techniques is very valuable. There are, however, some areas of caution.

Beware of evaluators who are full professors and rigorous in standards, rigid in procedures, and lecture all of the time. They may well suggest to the instructor that being "tough" works for them and that it is the "right" way to do things in the department, which can place the faculty member in a difficult position. To be very rigorous and rigid may lead to very low student ratings (which the full professor may currently receive). If student ratings are used heavily in promotion and tenure decisions, then faculty may find themselves being denied after following the sound advice of their colleagues.

Similarly, colleagues may explain that there is too much material to be covered by groupwork and the only legitimate method of instruction is lecture. My point here is that one is asking for assistance from individuals who, like the instructor, belong to a system. In seeking to improve teaching effectiveness one is making changes to that system and it is wise to understand the ripple effect of such changes.

Also be careful of receiving too much advice all at once. The person observing a class and reviewing teaching materials may give a lot of feedback. As with student ratings, focus on one or two items and begin the road to better teaching by adjusting those areas.

Conclusion

There are many sources of evaluation data that can be used to improve teaching effectiveness (e.g., Davis, 1993; McKeachie, 2005; Seldin & Associates, 1999). The most important factor in making a change is taking charge of the learning environment. Effective teaching is a lifelong pursuit. It is never considered accomplished and is best thought of as a system—as one aspect of the learning environment changes, so, too, will others. There is no one best way to teach and no one most effective personality for teaching. I have met faculty who have taught 30, 40, even 50 years and who still get excited every time they meet a new class. These same faculty are also constantly on the lookout for ways to use evaluation data to improve their teaching effectiveness.

REFERENCES

Atwater, L. E. (1998). The advantages and pitfalls of self-assessment in organizations. In J. W. Smither (Ed.), *Performance appraisal: State of the art in practice* (pp. 331–369). San Francisco, CA: Jossey-Bass.

Braskamp, L. A., & Ory, J. C. (1994). *Assessing faculty work: Enhancing individual and institutional performance.* San Francisco, CA: Jossey-Bass.

Clark, D. J., & Redmond, M. V. (1982). *Small group instructional diagnosis: Final report.* Washington, DC: Graduate School of Education and Human Development, The George Washington University. (ERIC Document Reproduction Service No. ED217954)

Davis, B. G. (1993). *Tools for teaching.* San Francisco, CA: Jossey-Bass.

McKeachie, W. J. (2005). *Teaching tips: Strategies, research, and theory for college and university teachers* (12th ed.). Boston, MA: Houghton Mifflin.

Seldin, P., & Associates. (1999). *Changing practices in evaluating teaching: A practical guide to improved faculty performance and promotion/tenure decisions.* Bolton, MA: Anker.

Wilson, P. F., & Pearson, R. D. (1995). *Performance-based assessments: External, internal, and self-assessment tools for total quality management.* Milwaukee, WI: American Society for Quality Press.

Using Evaluation Data for Personnel Decisions

12

David Fite

American colleges and universities now conduct more comprehensive and systematic faculty evaluation for personnel decisions than ever before. Both public and private institutions use an increasingly wide range of evidence and sources regarding faculty teaching, research and scholarship, and service in salary, contract renewal, retention, promotion, and tenure decisions. Most faculty evaluation systems feature use of multiple data sources and include faculty self-evaluation, student ratings, peer review, and reviews by the chair, dean, and faculty evaluation committees. By almost all measures, faculty evaluation in most American colleges and universities is substantially better than it was two decades ago when the first comprehensive faculty performance reviews were undertaken in higher education.

Barriers to Effective Faculty Evaluation

Yet substantial barriers to effective faculty evaluation remain in American higher education. The changing nature of higher education and the faculty workforce have created additional barriers to effective evaluation that present important challenges for the coming decades. The increasing numbers of part-time and adjunct faculty, now composing more than 50% of the faculty at many public universities (Cataldi, Bradburn, & Fahimi, 2005), present particular issues for evaluation. These faculty often teach in relatively unsupervised circumstances the lower-division, introductory, and service courses in many disciplines. Similar questions arise regarding the evaluation of the increasing numbers of nontenure-track full-time faculty hired to teach the same courses with differing expectations for teaching, research, scholarship, and service than their tenure-track colleagues. Finally, the growing percentage of tenured senior faculty members within the shrinking proportion of tenure-track faculty in American universities also raises questions about the uses of faculty evaluation and post-tenure review to maintain the vitality of senior faculty and an aging professoriate.

Other barriers to effective faculty evaluation include unclear definitions of the faculty roles of teaching, research, and scholarship, lack of faculty and institutional consensus on the values and relative weights assigned to faculty roles, and unclear and inconsistent evaluation processes and guidelines. These are related to two main obstacles to effective faculty evaluation seen by many commentators: faculty resistance and administrative apathy (Arreola, 2000; Theall, 2002).

Faculty resistance to evaluation arises for a number of reasons. First, as Arreola (2000) observes, no one likes being evaluated. But faculty have additional reasons for resistance to evaluation that include the problems of definition and process already mentioned. These problems remain especially acute in the area of teaching, where, despite advances in recent years, both faculty and those who evaluate them often lack specific training and professional expertise. In addition, serious technical and operational issues continue to plague faculty evaluation, especially when evaluation instruments of uncertain or poor psychometric quality are used or when information from valid instruments is misused or misinterpreted by faculty and administrators who lack training and expertise (Theall, 2002).

These problems only exacerbate a climate of faculty resistance based upon fear of unfair evaluation and ignorance of the substantial research affirming the validity and reliability of many commonly used instruments for evaluating teaching. Many faculty members continue to argue that students are not competent to evaluate them when research convincingly demonstrates those areas in which students are competent, such as delivery of instruction and availability of instructor, as well as the areas in which they are not, such as subject matter mastery and curriculum development (Seldin & Associates, 1999). Some faculty continue to believe that teaching is too complex an activity to be evaluated or measured. However, faculty are being evaluated all the time for their teaching and, by the same measure, they continually evaluate student learning and reduce it to a grade or a number.

Overcoming Barriers

Administrative support for faculty evaluation is especially important in the context of ongoing faculty resistance. The administration must actively support a comprehensive faculty evaluation system in order for it to succeed. This includes supporting the generally modest expenses required for an effective faculty evaluation program and welcoming the engagement of faculty in personnel decision-making processes.

An example will make clear the nature of the work required and the need for administrative support of faculty evaluation. The Faculty Personnel Council at my institution (Chapman University) is a seven-person faculty committee that reviews all university tenure and promotion cases as well as sabbatical and faculty development proposals. In the 2004–2005 academic year, the council reviewed and wrote evaluative letters regarding ten tenure cases, nine lateral hires with tenure, five promotions, and twenty-one third and fifth-year critical year reviews. The council also reviewed eleven sabbatical and faculty development leave proposals. For all tenure and promotion cases the council received a six-inch-thick multi-partitioned binder containing hundreds of pages of materials documenting faculty teaching, research, scholarship, and service as well as the reviews of department chairs, deans, local personnel committees, and external reviewers. Critical year reviews and lateral hires with tenure also required review of substantial if slightly less extensive documentation. It was estimated that the seven-member council reviewed nearly ten thousand pages of faculty personnel files during the academic year.

This daunting workload is common for college and university committees conducting faculty evaluation and suggests the level of commitment and expense of time required for each member, especially the chair. Add to this the important and deeply sensitive nature of the work done by such committees and you have reasons for appreciation of and concern for their work. The administration must actively support the work of faculty evaluation done by such committees, as it has at my university, and welcome the engagement of faculty. Administrators must also ensure that all involved receive the training and technical support they need in order for faculty evaluation to be undertaken fairly and effectively.

The Impact of Flawed Personnel Decisions

Support for effective faculty evaluation will help reduce flawed personnel decisions that are demonstrably destructive to faculty and institutions. Few kinds of decisions affect colleges and universities more than faculty personnel decisions. Personnel decisions impact the personal lives and professional careers of faculty, the morale and well-being of their colleagues and students, the programs and plans of their departments and colleges, and the culture and directions of their institutions. Personnel decisions reflect the changing roles of faculty and changing definitions of teaching, research, and scholarship. Flawed personnel decisions dramatize the tension between the stated principles and actual practices (and politics) of institutions. Flawed decisions may engage the college or university and the parties involved in a faculty evaluation dispute in time-consuming, labor-intensive, expensive, and stressful grievances and lawsuits.

Flawed personnel decisions undermine the necessary trust upon which faculty evaluation systems and well-functioning departments and institutions are built. They widen the adversarial gulf that already exists at many colleges and universities, especially those with a unionized faculty. Flawed personnel decisions affect other areas such as faculty governance by undermining faculty and administrator relations. They threaten the sense of shared purposes that underlie the complex yet fragile bonds of academic community and which support productive teaching, research, and student engagement. Ultimately, the perceived discrepancy between an institution's stated principles and actual faculty evaluation practices may affect the decisions faculty make about their own roles and workload and deflect the pursuit by faculty and academic programs of their institution's stated missions and educational goals.

The Role of the Courts in Faculty Evaluation

One of the most obvious impacts of flawed personnel decisions is to expose colleges and universities to grievances, litigation, and lawsuits. The number of employment discrimination cases and of tenure-denial cases in higher education has risen significantly in recent years (Franke, 2001). The courts have played an increasingly important role in faculty evaluation and personnel decisions since 1972 when Congress extended Title VII of the Civil Rights Act of 1964 to colleges and universities, prohibiting employers from discriminating on the basis of race, sex, color, national origin, and religion. In 1990 the Supreme Court ruled that university tenure reviews are not shielded by any special privilege from the general laws of evidence, which means that "confidential" views from tenure processes can be exposed to public and legal scrutiny. Another change in the law has taken employment discrimination cases out of the purview of judges and placed them in the hands of juries, who are regarded as more skeptical of institutions and sympathetic to the individual faculty member (Franke, 2001).

Fear of the courts and litigation has compelled colleges and universities to develop faculty evaluation methods that provide due process and are nondiscriminatory—that have clear procedures and performance standards and explicit criteria that use multiple sources and objective evidence and include stated reasons for decisions and formal appeals process, that are not discriminatory and do not use hearsay or any evidence not part of the evaluation process.

Fear of the courts and litigation has also arguably contributed to the burdensome expansion of faculty evaluation processes and materials, to off-putting legalism and bureaucratization of evaluation processes, to increased workload, demands, and stress on those involved in faculty evaluation processes, and to the misuse of evidence and overreliance on data and sources that offer the appearance of objectivity or lend themselves to quantification and ranking.

It will never be possible to ensure that all disputes arising from personnel decisions can be resolved within the institution. But following certain guidelines may help colleges and universities to minimize the possibility of legal complications in personnel decisions and ensure the fairness and equitability of faculty evaluation (Seldin, 1984; Seldin & Associates, 1999).

- Institutions must ensure that personnel decisions are not discriminatory in intent, process, or results.
- Institutions must provide criteria and procedures for faculty evaluation in writing and in detail to all faculty members.
- Institutions must provide specific and valid reasons in writing to faculty who receive negative decisions.
- The faculty evaluation system must include a formal appeals process.
- Institutions must evaluate faculty members on the basis of established performance standards and actual work assigned.

- Faculty evaluation systems should use multiple evaluation sources and pursue sources independently.

- Institutions must not allow the use of hearsay as evidence in any tenure, promotion, or retention decisions.

The days are long gone when private conversations between faculty and administrators could be used to provide an off-the-record view of a faculty member being evaluated. Today, word of that private discussion can be sufficient to cause an adverse ruling in court. Institutions must keep in mind that all oral and written comments that emerge from a faculty evaluation process can be used as evidence in a tenure-denial lawsuit (Franke, 2001).

Franke (2001) provides additional helpful recommendations for making defensible faculty evaluations and reducing the likelihood of litigation arising out of personnel decisions:

- Provide tenure-track faculty with honest evaluations of their work and prospects for tenure.

- Consider nonrenewal during the probationary period if appropriate.

- Be candid with a faculty member from the start about the strengths and deficiencies in his or her performance.

- Help individuals who have been denied tenure move on with their careers.

When a faculty member has received numerous positive evaluations in annual reviews and subsequently is denied tenure, an institution faces a difficult challenge in a grievance process or in court. A situation such as this represents a collective failure on the part of the faculty members and administrators charged with making honest evaluations and judgments. In particular, departments must resist the temptation to defer difficult judgments to campus committees or administrators or to a later stage of the evaluation process.

The Varied Importance of Teaching, Research, and Service

Faculty evaluation for personnel decisions generally focuses on the three central roles defining faculty work in the university: teaching, research and scholarship, and service. There are significant differences in the importance assigned to each role in different kinds of institutions. In addition, substantial changes have taken place over the past three decades in the ways these roles are defined and the kinds of evidence gathered for evaluating each.

Recent research on evaluation of faculty performance at American liberal arts colleges and universities shows that classroom teaching remains the most important factor in evaluation of overall faculty performance. Student advising and campus committee work are widely cited as important factors. Research and publication have risen significantly in importance in evaluation of faculty performance even at liberal arts colleges and universities (Seldin & Associates, 1999).

Faculty members at research-oriented universities understand that they will be judged primarily on the basis of their research and scholarship in personnel decisions. But faculty members at other kinds of institutions have become increasingly convinced (and concerned) that they are being judged primarily on the basis of their research and scholarship even when the stated mission of their institutions emphasizes the primacy of teaching. Faculty members at many institutions indicate that they do not clearly understand the performance standards and criteria by which they will be judged. A fair and effective faculty evaluation system must define teaching, research and scholarship, and service precisely and must clearly state their importance in relation to each other.

This does not mean that the institution must devise a formula for the relation between faculty roles. When revising its faculty manual several years ago, my university specifically rejected the traditional formula of 40:40:20 for calculating the relative weight of teaching, research and scholarship, and service. Such a formula does not account for the differences between individual faculty, types of faculty, career stages, specializations, and disciplines, nor does it recognize that faculty scholarly, professional, and creative work can take place across the roles of teaching, service, and outreach (Diamond, 2002).

Many institutions need to revise their faculty evaluation and reward systems to encompass more expansive and productive definitions of teaching, research, and service and to take into account new kinds of faculty work emerging in recent years. The work of curriculum development and reform, application of new technologies to instruction and curriculum, and development of learning outcomes assessment plans all need to be recognized in faculty evaluation systems if faculty are going to continue to undertake such activities. Faculty and student research and new forms of electronic scholarship as well as other forms of the scholarship of integration, application, and teaching also must be recognized and rewarded. Interdisciplinary and collaborative teaching, research, and scholarship must be recognized to reflect cutting-edge developments in departments, disciplines, and universities.

Faculty activities related to service have grown significantly in recent years with the development of service-learning and expansion of university outreach and public service. Similarly, the definition of service has been richly expanded at many colleges and universities through consideration of collegiality as an underlying value of the academic community and an emphasis on citizenship in departmental, institutional, regional, and disciplinary communities.

The Role of Objective Data and Subjective Personnel Decisions

The development of more systematic faculty evaluation making increased use of objective data represents welcome progress from faculty evaluation processes of previous years, which were too often subjective, arbitrary, private, and overreliant on opinion and hearsay. Objective data plays an important role in effective faculty evaluation systems. The use of such data generally ensures a more detailed, comprehensive picture of the wide range of activities that constitute teaching, research and scholarship, and service.

Yet the increased use of objective data also presents problems. It may blur the distinction between description and the more important task of evaluation of faculty work. Citing the number of articles a faculty member has published does not constitute an evaluation of the quality and significance of the faculty member's published work. Counting the number of committees on which a faculty member has served says little about the importance of those committees or of the faculty member's contribution to them. An overreliance on apparently objective data may lead to a reductive picture and distorted measurement of faculty work, which privileges quantification (what can be counted) over quality (what counts) in faculty work (Braskamp & Ory, 1994) (see Chapter 9).

This in turn only exacerbates the discrepancy that often exists between what faculty value in their work and what faculty evaluation processes measure (Braskamp & Ory, 1994). For example, faculty evaluation processes that rely almost exclusively on student ratings of teaching do not reflect the wide range of activities that faculty members understand to constitute effective teaching. The quantification of a single type of evidence through the use of composite scores or rankings from student ratings of teaching does not reflect the complexity of teaching. It is this complexity that makes the collection of a wide range of evidence about teaching even more important (Seldin, 1984).

Faculty evaluation relies inescapably on the subjective judgments of faculty, administrators, students, and others. A faculty evaluation system can never be wholly objective. Yet, as Arreola (2000) and others observe, the impact of subjectivity can and should be controlled in faculty evaluation systems. Effective faculty evaluation systems define and clarify the value structures implicit in faculty evaluation and the evidence used to evaluate faculty work. Effective faculty evaluation systems control subjectivity by using multiple types and sources of evidence, reflecting the complexity of faculty work. Effective faculty evaluation provides what Shulman (1988) calls "a union of insufficiencies, a marriage of complements, in which the flaws of individual approaches to assessment are offset by the virtues of their fellows" (p. 38).

Ultimately, faculty evaluation is the exercise of professional judgment regarding the quality of faculty work, not an objective science. This exercise of professional judgment relies on shared values, clearly communicated public norms, and fair, equitable, and transparent processes. Effective faculty evaluation provides reasons, presents evidence, and makes a case for the quality and significance of faculty work (Braskamp & Ory, 1994).

Multiple Data Sources

Experts on faculty evaluation agree on the importance of multiple data sources and the need for different kinds of evidence in the evaluation of faculty performance. Yet many institutions fail to follow the guidelines presented by experts to ensure that faculty evaluation fairly and accurately captures the multiple dimensions of faculty performance.

Recent research has shown that student ratings of teaching are now the most widely used source of information for evaluating teaching at American colleges and universities (Seldin & Associates, 1999). The use of student ratings has increased dramatically over the last 20 years. The use of three other sources of information about faculty teaching effectiveness has also increased significantly: faculty self-evaluation, peer classroom observation, and review of course syllabi and exams.

Too often student ratings are the only data used in summative evaluation of teaching for personnel decisions. Student ratings provide valuable information about students' perceptions of faculty teaching skills, organization of course materials, clarity of instructor presentation, teacher-student interaction, faculty availability, and student advising. But the information from student ratings must be combined with information from other sources such as faculty peers, chairs, deans, and faculty self-evaluation in order to develop a comprehensive view of the complex activities of teaching (see Chapter 4).

No other form of faculty evaluation has been subject to such a wide variety of misuses as student ratings of teaching, exacerbating the suspicions that many faculty members have of such ratings (see Chapter 10). Student ratings from a single course should never be used in faculty evaluation for personnel decisions. Nor should all the items or any single item be averaged into a single composite score. A principled faculty evaluation system will make thoughtful comparative judgments but will not make judgments about teaching effectiveness on the basis of statistically insignificant differences between a faculty member's ratings and an average for faculty in the institution, department, or discipline. Well-trained evaluators will take into account students' motivation when interpreting student ratings and will decide how to treat courses from different levels (freshman versus senior) and from different academic disciplines (humanities and social sciences versus mathematics and natural sciences) (Cashin, 1999). Student ratings should be used in faculty evaluation for personnel decisions to provide a comprehensive, longitudinal view of the faculty member's teaching effectiveness, in combination with a wide variety of other sources and evidence.

Though classroom peer observation is increasing in popularity, it remains a controversial (and debatable) source of information for personnel decisions. Poorly conducted classroom observation by untrained observers is unfair and may be injurious to the morale of the faculty member observed. Information from a single classroom observation should not be used in faculty evaluation for personnel decisions. Effective classroom observation requires precisely what is missing in many American colleges and universities: careful planning, appropriate training, and an atmosphere of open communication and mutual trust (see Chapter 6). More than any other source of information about faculty teaching, effective classroom peer observation requires a prior change in the culture of the institution away from the pedagogical solitude that Shulman (1993) describes as our dominant (and unproductive) tradition and toward a more productive notion of teaching as community property defined by Hutchings (1996) and others.

My university, like many, has adopted the use of teaching portfolios in recent years. The teaching portfolio offers a structured opportunity for faculty self-evaluation and for evidence-based reflection on the wide range of activities that constitute effective teaching (Seldin, 2004) (see Chapter 8). Self-evaluation should not be the primary source of information in judging teaching performance for personnel decisions. To adopt the use of teaching portfolios for summative faculty evaluation in personnel decisions is a potentially risky move without the substantial acculturation and faculty development support my university has provided, including the use of expert consultants, teaching portfolio workshops, individual counseling, and incorporation in new faculty orientation. Teaching portfolios are most effective when they are part of a shift in the culture of the institution promoting the evidence-based practice of teaching and the notion of teaching as community property.

The most common evidence used in evaluation of faculty research, scholarship, and creative activity includes scholarly books and monographs, textbooks, publication in professional journals, conference papers and presentations, and grants and sponsored research. A continuing difficulty for many colleges and universities is how to move from an evaluation of faculty research and scholarship that relies essentially on quantification, such as counting the number of articles in refereed journals, to one that addresses satisfactorily more substantive questions of quality. This problem is exacerbated by the difficulties faced by administrators and colleagues from disparate disciplines on university faculty evaluation committees who are reluctant to pass judgment on the quality of faculty work in other and often very different disciplines (see Chapter 9).

This challenge has been addressed through the use of external evaluators in personnel and tenure decisions who are asked to provide an assessment of the work of the faculty member in their discipline. Another approach to assessing the significance of scholarly work and research is the use of citation analysis, which focuses on how often a publication is cited by others in a specific period of time. Citation analysis is helpful in determining the impact or utility of scholarly work but must be used with caution due to serious methodological challenges and different citation patterns across fields and disciplines (Braskamp & Ory, 1994).

Many institutions have not yet incorporated into their faculty evaluation processes the groundbreaking work of Boyer (1990), Rice (1991), and others on defining and assessing faculty research and scholarship. These colleges and universities would do well to incorporate explicitly into their faculty evaluation processes the qualitative standards for scholarship presented in volumes such as *Scholarship Assessed* (Glassick, Huber, & Maeroff, 1997). These standards include clear goals, adequate preparation, appropriate methods, significant results, effective presentation, and reflective critique. Use of these standards will enable department chairs, administrators, and faculty committees to assess more effectively the quality of faculty research and scholarship and will promote more informed awareness and discussion among faculty and departments regarding the kinds and value of the work in which they are engaged.

A final point remains to be made about institutional uses of faculty evaluation data in personnel decisions. It is important that the institution develop evaluation processes that ensure high-quality data collection and management, timely and comprehensive analysis, and compilation of clear, useful reports. The manifold activities and daunting workload of faculty evaluation committees must be supported by standardized processes of data collection, a comprehensive database, secure files, and clear policies ensuring the confidentiality of faculty evaluation information (Theall, 2002).

Faculty Evaluation and Institutional Mission

As colleges and universities face increasing competition, public skepticism, and calls for accountability, it is more important than ever for all institutions to define a clear institutional mission and vision. They must then develop faculty evaluation systems that are consistent with their own clearly defined missions, educational goals, and values. Diamond (2002) presents the following characteristics of a mission-based faculty reward system:

- *Institutional priorities and mission must be directly supported by system criteria.* Faculty evaluation guidelines for promotion, tenure, and periodic review should clearly relate the criteria and importance assigned to faculty roles and activities to the institution's mission and central educational goals.

- *All institutional documents relating to faculty rewards should be consistent and integrated.* Academic units in a university such as mine whose core value is "personalized education" must develop faculty evaluation criteria and weightings consistent with a commitment to personalized education in faculty activities such as academic advising, mentoring, faculty-student collaboration and research, and capstone courses and senior seminars.

- *The faculty reward system should be sensitive to differences.* An effective faculty evaluation system should recognize different strengths of faculty, differences between the disciplines, and different missions and priorities in individual academic units. An effective faculty evaluation system must take into account the different strengths, interests, and contributions of different types of faculty and of faculty at different stages in their academic careers. A faculty evaluation system must take into consideration the substantial differences between disciplines with regard to the faculty roles of teaching, research and scholarship, and service. Effective faculty evaluation recognizes the distinctive goals and priorities of individual academic units, representing a wide variety of departments and disciplines, in serving the institution's mission and goals.

Guidelines for Effective Faculty Evaluation

There is widespread agreement on the guidelines for developing a system to evaluate overall faculty performance. These guidelines pertain to the development of the faculty evaluation program and to the characteristics of effective faculty evaluation.

Be Clear About the Purposes of the Faculty Evaluation System

It is important at the start to reach a clear and public understanding of the purposes of the faculty evaluation program. The program's purpose will determine the types of information gathered as well as the evaluation procedures. In particular, formative faculty evaluation to improve teaching and performance should be separated from summative faculty evaluation used to make personnel decisions. Faculty members who participate in good faith in faculty evaluation to improve their teaching, research, and service must not find that criticisms made for formative purposes are subsequently used against them when applying for retention, tenure, and promotion. Both formative and summative faculty evaluation are very important but should be kept separate. An institution should not introduce a faculty evaluation system whose purpose is formative and then gradually transform it into summative uses for personnel decisions (Seldin, 1984; Seldin & Associates, 1999; Theall, 2002).

Involve Faculty in the Development and Administration of Faculty Evaluation

The foundation of an effective faculty evaluation program is its acceptance by the faculty, who must have confidence in the evaluation program's integrity (Seldin & Associates, 1999). This means that faculty must have central roles in the development and administration of the program. Those involved in developing a faculty evaluation program must anticipate and respond to faculty resistance, including the legitimate concerns faculty have about faculty evaluation. The development of an evaluation system must be based on frank and open communication between faculty and administrators about faculty evaluation and should incorporate mechanisms for ongoing review and modification of the faculty evaluation system in response to problems that arise and faculty concerns and needs.

Educate Faculty and Administrators Involved in the Faculty Evaluation System

Faculty and administrative members of faculty evaluation committees should be given training and orientation in the form of a workshop at the beginning of every academic year on the research and practices of faculty evaluation. Faculty members and chairs of departments should be acquainted with resources such as *The Disciplines Speak* (Diamond & Adam, 1995, 2000), which presents statements on faculty work from more than 25 disciplines. Ultimately, education in faculty evaluation should be related to the development of an institutional culture of research-based practice in teaching, research, and service. This culture should promote faculty awareness of emerging emphases on teaching as community property and the scholarship of teaching and familiarity with new definitions of scholarship including the scholarship of integration and application as well as discovery. Faculty and institutional awareness of these trends should inform development of the uses of teaching portfolios in faculty evaluation processes.

Connect Faculty Evaluation to Faculty Mentoring and Development

Faculty members who receive recommendations or respond to criticisms presented as part of their periodic or annual reviews should find appropriate support and guidance from their chair and colleagues in their department or an institutional office of faculty development in order to address areas of concern in their teaching, research and scholarship, or service (see Chapter 3). A deeper point is that any faculty evaluation process should be placed in the larger context of a departmental and institutional culture that orients and supports tenure-track and nontenure-track faculty members from the time they are hired until they retire or leave the institution. This means, among other things, that faculty members must know what is expected of them. Many institutions require the submission of an annual proposal and report by each faculty member. An annual meeting with the department chair offers the opportunity to discuss expectations and clarify the criteria upon which the faculty member will be judged and to review progress in meeting agreed-upon performance standards. Faculty members who are deficient in one area or another should be told in annual or periodic reviews well before any possible decision to terminate them and should be offered the opportunity to improve their performance (Seldin & Associates, 1999).

An effective faculty evaluation system promotes faculty acculturation and development while representing and enforcing the expectations and ideals of the institution. Effective faculty evaluation both exemplifies and enables the sense of shared purposes and atmosphere of mutual trust that mark institutions in which the activities of teaching and learning, research and scholarship, and service are harmonized in support of their central mission and educational goals.

REFERENCES

Arreola, R. A. (2000). *Developing a comprehensive faculty evaluation system: A handbook for college faculty and administrators on designing and operating a comprehensive faculty evaluation system* (2nd ed.). Bolton, MA: Anker.

Boyer, E. L. (1990). *Scholarship reconsidered: Priorities of the professoriate*. Princeton, NJ: Carnegie Foundation for the Advancement of Teaching.

Braskamp, L. A., & Ory, J. C. (1994). *Assessing faculty work: Enhancing individual and institutional performance*. San Francisco, CA: Jossey-Bass.

Cashin, W. E. (1999). Student ratings of teaching: Uses and misuses. In P. Seldin & Associates, *Changing practices in evaluating teaching: A practical guide to improved faculty performance and promotion/tenure decisions* (pp. 25–44). Bolton, MA: Anker.

Cataldi, E. F., Bradburn, E. M., & Fahimi, M. (2005). *2004 National Study of Postsecondary Faculty (NSOPF:04): Background characteristics, work activities, and compensation of instructional faculty and staff: Fall 2003* (NCES 2006–176). Washington, DC: National Center for Education Statistics, U.S. Department of Education.

Diamond, R. M. (2002). The mission-driven faculty reward system. In R. M. Diamond (Ed.), *Field guide to academic leadership* (pp. 271–291). San Francisco, CA: Jossey-Bass.

Diamond, R. M., & Adam, B. E. (1995). *The disciplines speak I: Rewarding the scholarly, professional, and creative work of faculty*. Washington, DC: American Association for Higher Education.

Diamond, R. M., & Adam, B. E. (2000). *The disciplines speak II: More statements on rewarding the scholarly, professional, and creative work of faculty*. Washington, DC: American Association for Higher Education.

Franke, A. (2001, November/December). Making defensible tenure decisions. *Academe, 87*(6), 32–36.

Glassick, C. E., Huber, M. T., & Maeroff, G. I. (1997). *Scholarship assessed: Evaluation of the professoriate.* San Francisco, CA: Jossey-Bass.

Hutchings, P. (1996). *Making teaching community property: A menu for peer collaboration and peer review.* Washington, DC: American Association for Higher Education.

Rice, R. E. (1991). The new American scholar: Scholarship and the purposes of the university. *Metropolitan Universities Journal, 1*(4), 7–18.

Seldin, P. (1984). *Changing practices in faculty evaluation.* San Francisco, CA: Jossey-Bass.

Seldin, P. (2004). *The teaching portfolio: A practical guide to improved performance and promotion/tenure decisions* (3rd ed.). Bolton, MA: Anker.

Seldin, P., & Associates. (1999). *Changing practices in evaluating teaching: A practical guide to improved faculty performance and promotion/tenure decisions.* Bolton, MA: Anker.

Shulman, L. S. (1993, November/December). Teaching as community property: Putting an end to pedagogical solitude. *Change, 25*(6), 6–7.

Shulman, L. S. (1988, November). A union of insufficiencies: Strategies for teacher assessment in a period of educational reform. *Educational Leadership, 46*(3), 36–41.

Theall, M. (2002). Leadership in faculty evaluation. In R. M. Diamond (Ed.), *Field guide to academic leadership* (pp. 257–270). San Francisco, CA: Jossey-Bass.

The Professional Portfolio: Expanding the Value of Portfolio Development

13

John Zubizarreta

When challenged to write about new directions in portfolio development and additional benefits to implementing portfolio strategies in a faculty member's comprehensive professional growth, I realized just how deeply I have invested in portfolio thinking during the course of my own professional advancement. A deep commitment to reflection, documented and assessed performance, and collaborative peer mentoring—the salient features of any vital portfolio project—has characterized my work with teaching, administrative, and student learning portfolios. No other activity has had a more profound impact on my career than the power of portfolios to help me become a reflective, intentional, mindful teacher, administrator, and academic citizen.

Recently, I have returned to the core principles of portfolio development to capture the multiple, shifting facets of my career. The portfolio method of tying reflection to rigorous evidence and collaboration has enabled me to articulate and document a dynamic professional path that has included teaching, scholarship, service, administration, and more. The model process and document template advocated by Seldin (1993, 2004) have served me well in devising a way to think carefully about the diverse components of my professional development. The portfolio has helped me to clarify my philosophy of teaching, scholarship, service, and academic leadership as a coherent vision tied to selective but detailed evidence for practical advancement and ongoing positive assessment. In short, I now use my professional portfolio as a vehicle for personal enhancement, meaningful self-awareness, performance evaluation, integration of compound responsibilities, formulation of challenging goals, and continuous improvement.

The (R)evolution of Portfolios

The worldwide movement in higher education toward the use of portfolios for improvement of teaching and as a complement to comprehensive systems of evaluation is now at an unprecedented height (see Chapter 8). The portfolio is an integral, ubiquitous part of teaching enhancement and assessment in institutions all over the globe, and as the concept has grown, so has the interest in how the habits of reflection, selective documentation of performance, and supportive mentoring can be extended and applied to other dimensions of faculty work. How can portfolio strategies help faculty bring meaning to scholarship and service in the same way that portfolios have proven invaluable in strengthening teaching and making needs transparent for both formative assessments and summative evaluations? If faculty add administrative responsibilities to their complex academic journeys, how can the portfolio process offer a means for integrating the broad range of values, obligations, achievements, and goals of faculty work entwined with academic leadership?

Seldin and Higgerson (2002) addressed the latter issue with the application of teaching portfolio methodologies to the administrative portfolio, a tool enabling academic leaders to reflect on their philosophies of leadership and conscientiously provide real evidence of accomplishments, areas for improvement, and specific goals. The process is carefully guided by a collaborative mentor whose charge is to offer the scrutiny of peer review and the support and structure needed for transformational insights into essential questions of academic leadership.

The issue of how a portfolio can help a faculty member coherently integrate other dimensions of professional engagement besides teaching is one that I faced when my institution adopted a yearly merit review system for faculty evaluation. Already past the earlier hurdles of tenure and successive promotions to the highest faculty rank, I moved beyond thinking about a portfolio as a mechanism for reflective analysis and documentation of teaching or administration to viewing the portfolio as a way of examining the common themes among the traditional categories of teaching, scholarship, and service. How are (or are?) my teaching, scholarship, and service connected in a larger, purposeful, rewarding professional plan? How could I use portfolio strategies to discover the synergy inherent in my multifaceted professional endeavors and avoid submitting every year a fragmented case for teaching, scholarship, service, leadership, and other professional activities as isolated components of an annual review? Once again, my thinking about portfolios evolved, and I refashioned my work to embrace the idea of an inclusive yet succinct, manageable professional portfolio.

What Is a Professional Portfolio?

The professional portfolio is an evidence-based written document in which a faculty member reflects on, concisely organizes, and documents selective details of teaching, scholarship, service, leadership, and other professional responsibilities and achievements. Selectivity is important because the professional portfolio should not be construed as a huge repository of indiscriminate documentation but rather a judicious, critical, purposeful analysis of performance, evidence, and goals—the kind of reflection and keen scrutiny of achievement and future directions that leads to authentic professional development, meaningful assessment, and sound evaluation.

Most effective professional portfolios written as a wide profile of teaching, scholarship, and service are about 10 pages of narrative reflection complemented by a judiciously chosen bank of evidence arranged in supportive appendixes. Faculty are commonly held accountable as professionals for demonstrating achievement and growth in teaching, scholarship, and service—the fairly universal trio of domains in faculty evaluation systems—but each faculty member's profile is unique because of differences in purpose, disciplines, philosophies, styles, job assignments, institutional cultures, and other personal factors. Consequently, every portfolio has an individualized signature, and the information revealed, analyzed, and documented in the narrative and the appendix bears a unique stamp that personalizes the portfolio process and resulting product.

Nevertheless, given the hegemony of the tripartite standards for faculty evaluation in higher education, nearly all faculty professional portfolios address, among other possible choices, the following seminal areas of professional activity, though arrangements and priorities may vary from time to time depending on purpose and external requirements:

- Statement of professional responsibilities (e.g., teaching load, advising, internship supervisions, thesis mentoring, institutional leadership, leadership in professional organizations, coordination of college/community service projects)
- Philosophy of teaching, scholarship, and service (with a focus on how the three endeavors are integrated and interdependent, how each informs the others)
- Strategies and methods in professional accomplishments (including reflections on approaches to teaching, research/publication/creative performance, and institutional/professional/community service)
- Development of materials for professional effectiveness (e.g., teaching syllabi, classroom handouts, online lecture notes and study guides, assignments, scholarly web resources, workshop exercises, databases, lab software, conference presentation slides, civic group/local school/college trustees presentation packets)

- Products or outcomes of student learning, scholarship, and service functions

- Evaluations of performance (student course ratings, peer assessments of teaching, annual chair evaluations, sample reviews of research/publications/grants, letters of appreciation from institutional/professional/community sources)

- Awards, recognitions, prestigious appointments in teaching, scholarship, and service; invitations to present/publish in field, deliver keynote addresses, lead workshops; requests for consulting services

- Improvement efforts, professional development, personal growth (especially valuable when framed within the context of institutional mission and priorities)

- Short-term and long-term professional goals

This list of categories is suggestive rather than prescriptive, and each faculty member will adapt the areas to fit individual professional engagements and institutional requirements. My most recent draft of a professional portfolio addresses these categories in my own fashion and strives concisely to integrate the sometimes competing dimensions of my work, pulling together my teaching, scholarship, service, and leadership in a narrative of eight single-spaced pages organized by the following table of contents and identified appendixes:

FACULTY PROFESSIONAL PORTFOLIO
Spring 2006

John Zubizarreta
Professor of English
Director of Honors and Faculty Development
Columbia College

Table of Contents

1) Portfolio Preface and Rationale

2) Responsibilities

3) Philosophy of Professional Engagement: Teaching, Scholarship, Service

4) Faculty Identity and Academic Leadership as Professional Nexus

5) Evaluation and Improvement of Professional Performance

6) Significant Professional Initiatives and Achievements

7) Professional Development Goals

8) Appendixes

    A) Teaching Portfolio: Reflective Narrative

    B) Collaborative Scholarship

    C) Faculty/Administrative Service on Campus and in Professional Venues

    D) Faculty/Administrative/Professional Awards in Teaching, Scholarship, Service

    E) Curriculum Vitae

    F) Presentations, Publications, Keynotes on Improving College Teaching, Learning, and Academic Leadership

    G) Consulting Materials

    H) Role and Responsibilities of Dean of Undergraduate Studies, Director of Honors and Faculty Development

    I) Workshops for Professional Development

    J) Communications With Faculty, Students, and Administrators; Commendations, Acknowledgements From Professional Sources

    K) Evidence of Professional Collaborations and Faculty/Student Collaborative Research

    L) Professional Improvement Efforts

M) Evaluations and Feedback: Student Ratings, Peer Reviews, Annual Evaluations, Professional Publications Reviews, Conference Presentation/Workshop/Consulting Feedback

N) Sharing Professional Insights and Recommendations: Letters Written for Colleagues and Students

Regardless of purpose and items that individualize each portfolio, the narrative body of the portfolio offers a faculty member an opportunity to reflect on key questions that nourish vigorous, successful professional development.

- What are your clear responsibilities as a professional in an increasingly complex and demanding professoriate?

- How do you go about your complicated work to meet the challenges of your multiple roles? What are your professional work strategies and priorities?

- What tools, materials, designs, and devices have you developed and used to help accomplish your work effectively?

- What evidence do you have of professional expertise, efficacy, and vitality?

- How are your professional endeavors reviewed by others?

- What are you doing for continuous professional improvement and growth?

Notice that the reflective process at the heart of professional portfolio development is a mirror of the same process used in institutional strategic planning and assessment: We identify the mission or philosophy of the institution, we study how well programs implement mission and goals, we examine evidence of efforts and achievements in programs, we see where improvements have been made or are needed, and we posit goals for the future. In a sense, then, portfolio development is strategic planning on the individual, professional level. It is a comprehensive articulation of mission or philosophy, a current assessment of competencies, a statement of objectives, a map of how to achieve improved performance, and a bank of supportive documentation. Developed as a digital production in electronic media, individual professional portfolios can establish instantaneous, seamless connections with departmental and institutional assessment and improvement projects. This is the kind of planning that results in clearer acknowledgements of professional purpose, better communication among faculty and administrators, and more supportive, constructive processes of professional evaluation and rewards.

Most importantly, however, the professional portfolio—whether on paper, on disk, or online—stimulates faculty to ponder an array of profound, value-laden *why* questions: *why* we teach; *why* we work as we do; *why* we choose certain priorities in teaching, scholarship, and service; *why* we publish in this or that field or particular topic; *why* our evaluations are affirming or disheartening; *why* teaching is more fulfilling than research or research more practically rewarding than teaching or service; *why* an administrative or other role in the profession is a positive challenge or a frustrating drain; *why* a profession in higher education is a positive vocation or a routine job. The emphasis on reflection—on constructing not only a coherent, penetrating, meaningful inquiry into *what we do* and *how we do it* but also an essential philosophy of *who we are* as faculty professionals—is a fundamental, critical process culminating in an act of writing that has its own intrinsic worth in enriching our professional identity and clarifying new and satisfying directions.

The Importance of Coherence, Unity, and Connections

The professional portfolio must demonstrate explicit coherence among the various components of its reflective portion by exploring the connections between philosophy—the core of the portfolio—and the different areas highlighted in the narrative's table of contents. In the most recent version of my professional portfolio, I have adapted previous drafts of reflective writing on the interplay between my values as a teacher and my work as a scholar and academic citizen in the profession and in the community. In the philosophy section of the portfolio, the vital heart of the process, after articulating a philosophy of teaching and how it serves as the hub of my entire professional career, I move on to use contemporary revaluations of scholarship and service to organize my thinking about how I try to integrate my diverse professional roles. Rather than separate teaching philosophy from scholarship and service as isolated entities, I borrow from Boyer (1990) the language I need to offer an integrated vision of my identity and purpose as a faculty professional. Here is an excerpt from the portfolio's sections on scholarship and service in my personal philosophy statement:

Scholarship

The professor must demonstrate competency and currency by actively engaging in the public, professional venues of scholarly publications and presentations at professional conferences. The *scholarship of teaching* is a crucial dimension of change in higher education, and it should complement and enrich the traditional arena of disciplinary research and publication as appropriate expressions of the necessary *scholarship of discovery* and *integration*, the kinds of professional work that indicate and validate expertise among communities of scholars. Such charges are seminal in fulfilling the responsibility of tenure (**Appendix B** in my portfolio contains published additional comments on the interaction between scholarship and teaching, and **Appendix F** has selected samples of scholarship related to fostering a climate of professional collaboration and reflective practice on my own and other college campuses). With two recent books, several periodical publications and chapters, and numerous papers and conference presentations in my home discipline of English and in other fields of faculty development and honors education, I have tried to live out my view that such scholarly work is essential to my role as an academic professional (Appendix E includes a record of scholarship in my *Curriculum Vitae*).

Service

The professor is also responsible for meeting the obligations of *academic citizenship*, for participating fully in faculty governance, for engaging meaningfully in institutional priorities and goals, for contributing to one's profession and the larger community. Faculty must be committed to pursuing the *scholarship of application* in addition to providing services to community groups and projects: The first mandate depends upon and expands the professor's disciplinary expertise through practical, professional service, and the latter promotes good will and positive, strong bonds between higher education and the community.

I believe I have lived up to my own values and performance standards in teaching, scholarship, and service. In this comprehensive professional portfolio, I demonstrate my passion for the classroom and my strong commitment to close contact with students, to innovation, to the collaborative act of learning that inspires both teacher and student, to rigorous scholarship, to working across disciplines with colleagues and students, to continuous professional development, and to service. The portfolio connects my roles as teacher, scholar, administrator of two academic programs, and active professional. References to evidence supporting my reflections are integrated throughout the portfolio and collected in the appendix.

Notice how the philosophy component of the portfolio is heavily loaded with values and beliefs, the kinds of priorities that should drive the decisions I make about what, how, and why I teach; what kinds of scholarship, research, and publications I pursue and why; as well as when, how, and why I engage in professional development activities such as faculty governance or organizational leadership. In other words, philosophy prompts us to work from a mindful, conscientious, perhaps even a courageous center: We become reflective practitioners, professionals. Given the depth of reflection involved and the challenge of trying to connect *who* we believe we *are* with *what* we *do* and its impact on others and our fields, it is no wonder that discovering and articulating a professional philosophy is often the most difficult step in portfolio development.

In addition to tying philosophy and practice in the narrative, the portfolio must also bridge the personal and powerful reflective nature of the narrative and the concrete documentation in the appendix. The integrated parenthetical references to various appendixes in the sample excerpt provide a good example of how an author can systematically connect claims, descriptions, and other rhetoric in the narrative to the organized, hard evidence necessarily collected in the appendix. Both forms of coherence—1) unity of philosophy and practice in the reflective narrative, and 2) consistent, transparent connections between the narrative and documentation—are central to the integrity of the portfolio and to establishing a reliable base of information for both improvement and evaluation purposes.

Portfolios and Professions: Works in Progress

Professional portfolios, just like professions themselves, are works in progress. We begin our professional lives in earnest, eager to advance in our fields, ready to accept new intellectual challenges, wanting to make a difference in our students' learning, our institutional cultures, our disciplinary organizations, our communities (see Chapter 7). As we navigate tenure, promotions, new responsibilities, shifting scholarly interests, changing institutional priorities, and the altered seasons of professional life, the professional portfolio emerges as a living document, growing with time in richness, scope, and complexity.

But in actual practice, the portfolio as product does not exceed its originally succinct format. As new materials are added, old ones are deleted. In fact, one of the ways in which the portfolio is comprised of selective information is that both the narrative and the appendixes are focused on relatively current accounts of one's responsibilities, philosophical values, methodologies, evaluations, goals, and other features of portfolio development. The end product remains consistently concise over time and multiple revisions. I generally urge portfolio authors to keep their documents confined to one- or two-inch binders, never more. Of course, electronic media open up an array of other possibilities for creating an increasingly sophisticated web of linked information, but one still should be careful about excess and the lure of digital glitz over selective substance.

How often should a faculty member revise a professional portfolio? I recommend a fresh reconsideration of the portfolio every year, perhaps at the end of the academic calendar. If one has taken advantage of the ready-made repositories of stored documentation in the portfolio's appendix, then finding new information for revisions is an easy task. Throughout the year, as new professional opportunities, assignments, achievements, bits of evidence, and insights emerge, the faculty member can simply store the items in the appropriate section of the portfolio for later review. In this way, the professional portfolio remains current and dynamic, reflecting a vigorous, engaged professional career. Such diligence in maintaining the currency of the portfolio allows for timely selection of parts or versions of the portfolio for varying purposes such as departmental or institutional assessment, supporting information for a grant proposal, tenure and promotion considerations, or new position applications. A revised, updated portfolio is always ready at hand for multiple purposes. For a list of specific strategies for updating the portfolio, I recommend a list of tips I developed for faculty maintaining teaching portfolios, a list adapted slightly to make it equally useful for more comprehensive professional portfolios (Zubizarreta, 2004).

- Use the appendix as a convenient, self-defined filing system for hardcopy information and documentation. For example, the portfolio should have an appendix for materials such as teaching handouts, recent publications, or evidence of new professional service responsibilities or awards. As new materials are acquired in the areas of teaching, scholarship, service, or other areas, place them into the appropriate appendix for future assessment.

- Don't reinvent the wheel. If year-end self-reports are part of one's evaluation system, then combine the narrative revision of the portfolio and its assessment of quantitative information in the appendix with the required report. Find ways of making required assessment and evaluation activities integral dimensions of portfolio revisions.

- Focus on selected areas for enhancement. Narrow the scope of improvement efforts and the amount of information analyzed in a revision. One year, for instance, concentrate on teaching: Identify one particular assignment in one course and the role of the teacher's periodic, written feedback on the work of three students of varying abilities. Next year, work on scholarship: Describe a new research and publication agenda and the challenges and achievements of reaching into new intellectual territory and the value to teaching and professional growth. Over time, the portfolio will become a living record of an engaged, vigorous professional journey without excessive time demands for revision.

- Keep revisions detailed and specific. Conceiving of revision as a complete reshaping of all the fundamental components of a professional portfolio is intimidating and unnecessary. Rarely do we undergo such dramatic revelations about philosophy and practice that the entire portfolio must be recast. Remember that the portfolio is a *process of continual analysis and improvement.* Revise deliberately, a step at a time.

- Take advantage of faculty development staff to help identify areas for improvement and suggest specific revisions of portions of the portfolio. Faculty developers can introduce new modes of analyzing our practice which may prompt ideas for revisions of the professional portfolio. In addition, many faculty development programs also offer support for research, publication, creative endeavors, grant writing, enhancement of academic leadership skills, issues of balancing career demands, and other factors in professional development.

- Entrust a mentor to help guide the development of a portfolio through its various revisions. While collaboration with an experienced colleague outside one's institution is often best in the initial stage of writing a professional portfolio, teaming with a knowledgeable peer within or outside the department or with a department chair can help create a useful perspective on the portfolio that stimulates worthwhile revision.

Professional Staff Portfolios

The value of professional portfolios extends beyond the faculty realm to include administration and support staff. With the growing interest in comprehensive institutional quality enhancement, driven by increasing pressures from accrediting bodies for colleges and universities to examine carefully and systematically the effectiveness of all academic and auxiliary units, many schools are encouraging and supporting the development of professional portfolios among staff members. Staff portfolios complement faculty, administrative, and student learning portfolios to form an interconnected network of information useful for both individuals and the institution to measure quality and plot positive change. Perhaps most important, the wide implementation of portfolio strategies across an entire campus results in a community dedicated to reflection, assessment, collaboration, and improvement.

Some campuses have already launched professional portfolios across all their constituents. The John A. Dutton e-Education Institute at Pennsylvania State University, for example, provides portfolio resources and models for faculty, staff, and students. The University of Denver Portfolio Community is another example of a flexible portfolio system designed to offer faculty, administrators, staff, and students an opportunity to archive their achievements, identify both secure and public areas of their work, use individually tailored rubrics to improve and evaluate their work, share assessment of their work for institutional research purposes, and (in the case of students) even continue to maintain portfolios as alumni of the college. An escalating trend in the commercial sphere is the number of providers who are designing portfolio software packages for institutional use by faculty, staff, and students alike. One example is the Open Source Portfolio Initiative used by Portland State University or the Chalk & Wire Professional Development e-Portfolio system used by Oral Roberts University. Of course, there are many in-house, institutionally developed programs. These are just some illustrations among a plethora of growing systems for professional portfolio development.

Professional Portfolios and the Future

The professional portfolio is not the only means of describing and documenting professional engagement and growth, but it is the only instrument I know that simultaneously helps us assess and evaluate our performance as teachers, scholars, academic citizens, or administrators; nourishes our professional identity and vision; and improves our professional work and influence through the process of reflection combined with rigorous assessment and collaborative mentoring. In developing a portfolio, we are empowered to think about our professional priorities, accomplishments, disappointments, and dreams; the choices we make daily to achieve our best work and contributions to our institutions and disciplines; the burdens and triumphs of finding integration and coherence among the diverse responsibilities of teaching, scholarship, service, and other endeavors; and the challenge of finding balance in our professional and personal lives.

Such reflection and coached analysis of the evidence of our professional efficacy are vital components of professional success and personal growth. The portfolio's process of written reflection invokes the power of narration and contextualization, the ability of writing to make the often unrecognized dimensions of our profession visible and understood by a community. In becoming reflective practitioners, we are more intentional in generating evidence of attainment and articulating needs for improvement. We are alive and dynamic, forward-looking, self-aware, and confident in our careers. We have tapped the power of the professional portfolio and are ready to move into a more sharply focused, more fulfilling professional future.

REFERENCES

Boyer, E. L. (1990). *Scholarship reconsidered: Priorities of the professoriate.* Princeton, NJ: Carnegie Foundation for the Advancement of Teaching.

Seldin, P. (1993). *Successful use of teaching portfolios.* Bolton, MA: Anker.

Seldin, P. (2004). *The teaching portfolio: A practical guide to improved performance and promotion/tenure decisions* (3rd ed.). Bolton, MA: Anker.

Seldin, P., & Higgerson, M. L. (2002). *The administrative portfolio: A practical guide to improved administrative performance and personnel decisions.* Bolton, MA: Anker.

Zubizarreta, J. (2004). Strategies for updating and improving the teaching portfolio. In P. Seldin, *The teaching portfolio: A practical guide to improved performance and promotion/tenure decisions* (3rd ed., pp. 112–117). Bolton, MA: Anker.

Summary and Recommendations for Evaluating Faculty Performance

14

J. Elizabeth Miller

This book provides a broad range of practical strategies for evaluating faculty performance. The following summary of key points and recommendations, reviewed here chapter by chapter, shows how successful evaluation programs may be implemented and enhanced.

Chapter 1: Building a Successful Evaluation Program
Peter Seldin

- There is no perfect system of faculty evaluation. Although performance appraisal is an art involving value judgment, with time, effort, and goodwill, reasonable approximations are reachable.

- Evaluation is a complex and evolving process and no single source of data is adequate. The combined appraisals of students, colleagues, administrators, and the professor's self-assessment are required for reasonable judgments.

- Fairness requires that the criteria, standards, and evidence used by an institution are disseminated clearly, fully, and in writing to every faculty member.

- Faculty performance improves when a professor can turn to trusted and respected faculty colleagues or instructional improvement specialists to interpret the ratings and discuss specific strategies for improvement.

- Many faculty members have legitimate fears that evaluation data gathered for improvement purposes will be abused by misapplication to tenure, promotion, and retention decisions.

- Many professors find it awkward and uncomfortable to appraise the performance of their peers. They can benefit from training in observation and in gathering evaluation data.

- Faculty evaluation programs must be administratively manageable and cost and time efficient.

- The cornerstone of any evaluation program is its acceptance by the faculty, which depends in turn on the faculty's confidence in the program's relevance, utility, and integrity.

Chapter 2: Essential Operating Principles and Key Guidelines
Peter Seldin

- Process is at least as important as product. It takes less time to touch base than it does to mend fences. Evaluation systems are produced by people who want to be consulted in determining how things will be done that impact them.

- To soften faculty resistance, experience suggests that sufficient time—a year or even two years—should be allowed for acceptance and implementation of the revised faculty evaluation program.

- It is wise to allow room for individual differences in the development of evaluation criteria, as long as these differences can be tolerated by the institution. Too often, colleges and universities center attention on the fine points of methodology rather than the criteria.

- There must be a clear linkage between the evaluation program and academic rewards. If the process produces only negative consequences, it is inviting failure. What good is a system that produces only faculty resentment?

- All faculty members must know the performance standards by which they will be evaluated. Specifically, they must know what constitutes exemplary, satisfactory, and unsatisfactory performance. Additionally, they must know what criteria and weights will be used for their evaluation.

- The primary purpose of the evaluation process should be to improve the quality of faculty performance, and its approach should be positive rather than punitive. The process should be based on a solid belief in maintaining the strengths and shoring up the weaknesses of each faculty member.

Chapter 3: Building a Climate for Faculty Evaluation That Improves Teaching
Mary Lou Higgerson

- Engage faculty in performance *counseling* instead of performance *evaluation* to make it more appealing to faculty. Performance counseling thwarts the natural inclination of faculty to become defensive when they or their work is criticized.

- Make teaching an institutional priority. Faculty who recognize that student learning is important are better able to document academic and institutional quality. When teaching becomes a campus priority, institutional success is demonstrated through assessment and teaching improvement activities.

- Create a context for performance counseling that is faculty-centered. When faculty believe that they benefit personally from performance counseling, they more willingly participate in assessment of their teaching. Set concrete and specific performance expectations. Ambiguity undermines the climate for performance counseling because it can be demoralizing and discouraging if there are few positive recognitions or results.

- Establish expectations for continuous review. When the counseling of teaching improvement becomes a year-round activity rather than a yearly event, the anxiety that may occur with more formal teaching evaluations is reduced.

- Recognize and support improvement. Faculty are more likely to sustain improvement when the institution recognizes and celebrates their effort and success.

Chapter 4: Uses and Abuses of Student Ratings
William Pallett

- Student ratings are a valuable resource but there are important elements of teaching that students are not well equipped to address. Student ratings should count 30% to 50% in the overall evaluation of teaching.
- Don't make too much of too little. Categorize student ratings results into no more than three to five groups (e.g., "Outstanding," "Exceeds Expectations," "Meets Expectations," "Needs Improvement but Making Progress," and "Fails to Meet Expectations"). Utilizing more categories will almost certainly exceed the measurement sophistication of the instrument being used.
- Student ratings instruments can serve multiple purposes. Be clear about the instrument's purposes and be certain that its content matches those purposes. If the survey is intended to serve multiple purposes (e.g., both personnel evaluation and teaching improvement), it will be longer than one intended to serve a single purpose.
- A good instrument can guide faculty improvement efforts and support program assessment. Instruments that focus on student learning and varied teaching methods can be used for both individual and programmatic improvement.
- If student ratings results are published, allow new instructors to establish a track record before circulating their ratings. Waiting two to three years for faculty to hone their teaching skills before facing public scrutiny seems a fair compromise.

- If an online student ratings system is used, do everything possible to obtain a response rate of 65% or higher. This will require constant monitoring and the implementation of various strategies to encourage students to respond.

Chapter 5: Institutional Service
Clement A. Seldin

- Service should benefit the department, institution, profession, agencies, or organizations.

- Faculty should read handbooks carefully and talk directly with their administrators and colleagues to clarify how institutional service is valued by the department, college, or university.

- Faculty should engage in both internal and external service that reflects the department's and institution's perspective on service and what is appropriate and important.

- When documenting service contributions, faculty should provide detail and evidence of active engagement. A brief description of the contribution, goals, and accomplishments is desirable. Committee reports or executive summaries as well as letters of support/appreciation from committees, organizations, and individuals should be cited in faculty reports (e.g., annual review, tenure, reappointment, and promotion). Artifacts should be included in an appendix.

- Leadership positions should be identified and described. This includes leadership on internal and external committees and subcommittees, elected or appointed positions on local, state, national, and international boards, for professional conferences, and academic journals.

- Faculty should keep ongoing records of all service. It is easy to maintain a computer file on institutional service and update it regularly. In addition, keep a file in a cabinet for any hard documents, reports, emails, letters, or certificates relating to specific service activities. When reviewed, it will be a far easier task to assemble a compelling case for substantial institutional service with details and solid evidence.

Chapter 6: Peer Observations as a Catalyst for Faculty Development

Barbara J. Millis

- Collegial peer observations are an effective strategy to improve teaching.

- The basic process of conducting effective peer observations is well documented in the literature. Observers should meet initially with the faculty member to be visited to discuss key logistic and pedagogical considerations; conduct the visit following guidelines that were previously agreed upon; incorporate a post-observation feedback session, including any written analysis; and provide feedback that reinforces positive teaching behaviors and the knowledge and motivation to change in positive ways.

- In addition to fostering department collegiality and strengthening teaching, peer observations can also foster the scholarship of teaching and learning.

- Both the observer and the person observed can benefit from peer visits, including the shared reflections.

- Departments that develop a common observation instrument can benefit from increased collegiality. The process of discussing and developing an observation instrument can also serve as a powerful faculty development tool.

- Three useful models for involving departments in the design of a common department observation instrument are traditional, participatory, and innovative.

Chapter 7: Self-Evaluation
Thomas V. McGovern

- Using an academic life narrative method, faculty members' reflections can lead to self-determined renewal and continuing self-evaluation.

- Erikson and Erikson's (1997) topography of psychological, epigenetic conflicts is an apt map for faculty members' development. McAdams's (2001) life story model of identity provides a reflective structure for such mapping.

- Faculty members continually recalibrate the balances between teaching, scholarship, and service commitments across the academic lifespan in keeping with their personal goals and the context of specific institutional environments.

- Reflective prompts may cover the range of undergraduate study identifications to the later stages of academic life. These serve as guides for goal-setting, faculty discussions, and the composition of an academic life narrative.

Chapter 8: Teaching Portfolios
Monica A. Devanas

- A teaching portfolio is a statement of a faculty member's teaching responsibilities, accomplishments as a teacher, and a self-reflection on his or her teaching philosophy. Eight to ten pages in length, it is supported by an appendix that contains course materials, student work, and assessments of teaching.

- A key component of the teaching portfolio is the teaching philosophy statement. In this section, faculty members describe their reasons for becoming a teacher, why they teach the way they do, and their motivation for teaching.

- The evidence section includes materials that document teaching effectiveness. Brief descriptions of materials are included here, while the actual artifacts are included in an appendix.

- Balance information and documentation from multiple sources in a teaching portfolio. Materials from the professor (e.g., course descriptions, a reflective statement, and course materials) are supplemented with documentation from students, peers, and colleagues in other departments or institutions.

- A mentor is the best assistance one can have in completing a teaching portfolio. A mentor can provide feedback on the clarity of the materials, connections between statements in the philosophy and course activities and assignments, other teaching activities, or suggestions for supporting evidence.

- The time and effort it takes to complete a portfolio are important investments in a faculty member's career. The teaching portfolio should be reviewed as frequently as a curriculum vitae is revised. The portfolio reflects the significant body of work in teaching and provides evidence for a faculty member to document his or her teaching effectiveness.

Chapter 9: Evaluating Faculty Research
Teck-Kah Lim

- A rigorous process for evaluating faculty research includes methods that account for the audience, the kind of researcher or group being evaluated, the type of outputs, outcomes, or impacts being measured, the period involved in the research, and the environment in which the research is conducted.

- Anthropological study is necessary for reliable assessments and evaluation. A fair-minded and educated evaluator should appreciate what research is, consider the human element in it, know its form and practice, and be able to place it in the context of the mission of an institution.

- Evaluators must have a reasonable idea of how research is practiced in different disciplines. Evaluators should understand the behavior patterns, mores, and cultures of researchers they are evaluating.

- Research focused on the scholarship of teaching and learning (i.e., a teacher who studies his or her practices) falls under the big tent of educational research. Researchers might engage in questioning, exploring, devising a strategy, executing it, testing, analyzing, and sharing the results.

- Quantitative performance indicators for research should form a discussion of the practices of research and the importance of various factors. These indicators may be appropriate criteria when a researcher is up for tenure or promotion.

- The greater the variety of measures and qualitative processes used to evaluate research, the greater the likelihood that a composite measure offers a reliable understanding of the knowledge produced. Those of us who evaluate research want measures of quality and productivity that will not fail us. Both bibliometric indicators and peer review have a place in the process.

Chapter 10: Teaching Evaluation Follies
Jane S. Halonen, George B. Ellenberg

- Student evaluations of teaching are a fact of life, but enormous foolishness too often characterizes practices by students, faculty, and administrators. With careful consideration, thoughtful design, and implementation with integrity, student evaluations can offer a critical piece of information to facilitate the evolution of a learning-centered campus.

- Clarify how and why student evaluations are conducted when students are asked to respond. This will improve data collection and increase its validity.

- Adopt a reflective approach to improving teaching. This will help faculty develop their own strategies to enhance their skills. Faculty who genuinely care about class quality will ask evaluative questions during the course rather than at the end when it is too late to change. Focusing on improvement will serve the faculty well during personnel evaluation decisions.

- Wise administrators will put teaching evaluation ratings in the larger context of the patterns that emerge across departments. They will take into account characteristics of the course, seasoning of the faculty member, and other variables that should constrain our interpretations.

- Student evaluations of teaching must never be used as the sole index of a faculty member's accomplishment. Syllabus construction, exam design, assignment development, peer visits, and/or videotape analysis can all provide useful, additional evaluation data.

- Students can be unduly harsh in their feedback. Teaching supervisors should develop strategies to contextualize such comments so faculty can extract ideas for improvement with minimal pain.

Chapter 11: Using Evaluation Data to Improve Teaching Effectiveness
Todd Zakrajsek

- Be mindful of one's status within the academy when using evaluation data to improve performance. Advice given for seasoned professors is often very different from advice for new faculty. Similarly, advice is often different for tenured faculty versus untenured faculty.

- Self-assessment is an important place to begin when seeking to improve teaching effectiveness. It is particularly helpful for those eager to change and those willing to take responsibility for their own behavior and how that behavior impacts student learning.

- Although student feedback is usually obtained at the end of the semester, it is even more valuable when gathered during the semester. Keep in mind that this data is based on perceptions of teaching.

- Employ colleagues to help improve teaching. In addition to observing classes and providing suggestions, they can also review teaching materials and provide guidance on materials such as the syllabus, examinations, grading rubrics, extra-credit assignments, and amount of material covered in a course.

- Obtain feedback on teaching from as many sources as possible and as often as possible. Multiple sources of evaluation data allow for a more comprehensive view of teaching and more possibilities for making improvements.

- Start small, working on only one or two key aspects of teaching at a time. Expect setbacks from time to time, as not all new strategies will work in all situations.

Chapter 12: Using Evaluation Data for Personnel Decisions
David Fite

- Effective faculty evaluation programs rely on established and widely understood performance standards and criteria. They evaluate faculty on the basis of performance across the years of the evaluation period and across the span of the activities that constitute effective teaching, research and scholarship, and service.

- Effective faculty evaluation programs use multiple evaluation sources and different types of evidence and do not rely on a single type of evidence such as student ratings of faculty teaching. They ensure fair and accurate interpretation and use of results.

- Effective programs provide due process, including standardized evaluation procedures, written reasons for negative personnel decisions, and a clearly defined appeals process. They ensure that institutions are consistent in conducting tenure processes and making tenure decisions.

- Effective programs feature high-quality data collection and analysis, timely and comprehensive analysis, and compilation of clear, useful reports. They include standardized processes of data collection, a comprehensive database, secure files, and clear policies ensuring the confidentiality of information.

- Institutions must be clear about the purposes of the faculty evaluation system. Formative evaluation used to improve teaching and performance should be separated from summative evaluation used to make personnel decisions.

- Institutions should engage faculty in the development and administration of faculty evaluation. Additionally, institutions should educate faculty and administrators involved in the evaluation system.

- Institutions should connect evaluation to faculty mentoring and development. Faculty evaluation should be part of an institutional culture that orients and supports faculty from the time they are hired until they retire or leave the university.

- Effective evaluation programs are based on an informed understanding of the research and best practices for faculty evaluation in higher education.

Chapter 13: The Professional Portfolio
John Zubizarreta

- The professional portfolio is an evidence-based written document in which a faculty member reflects on, concisely organizes, and documents selective details of *teaching, scholarship, service, leadership, and other professional responsibilities and achievements.*

- The portfolio stimulates an array of profound, value-laden *why* questions: *why* we teach; *why* we work as we do; *why* we choose certain priorities in teaching, scholarship, and service; *why* higher education is a positive vocation or a routine job; and others. The emphasis on reflection—on constructing not only a coherent, penetrating, meaningful inquiry into *what we do* and *how we do it* but also an essential philosophy of *who we are* as faculty professionals—is a fundamental, critical process.

- The professional portfolio bridges reflection and concrete documentation in the appendix, systematically connecting claims, descriptions, and other rhetoric in the narrative to organized, hard evidence. Such coherence is central to the integrity of the document and to establishing a reliable base of information for both improvement and evaluation purposes.

- The professional portfolio is more than a personnel file, annual report, or similar product. It is an ongoing process of reflection, documentation, and collaborative mentoring that offers an opportunity to integrate the various, often competing dimensions of professional engagement in higher education.

- The value of professional portfolio development extends beyond faculty to include administration, support staff, and students. With growing interest in comprehensive institutional quality enhancement, many colleges and universities are encouraging and supporting portfolio strategies to enhance teaching, learning, leadership, and staff advancement. The wide implementation of portfolio strategies across an entire campus results in a community dedicated to reflection, assessment, collaboration, and improvement.

Appendix

Selected Forms to Evaluate Teaching, Advising, Research, and Service

Instead of creating original faculty evaluation forms, most colleges and universities can benefit from the models already developed elsewhere. The rating forms, of course, must be congenial in nature and content with the goals of a particular college or university. Selection of the questionnaire items will depend on local conditions as well as institutional and department objectives. In general, it is wiser to adapt—not adopt—an already existing model and reshape it to meet local conditions and needs.

Twelve field-tested and widely used forms for evaluating faculty performance in teaching, advising, research, and service are presented in this appendix. They should not be considered as the definitive word, but rather as a starting point for campus discussion intended to mold and reshape the forms for a better fit with institutional or departmental needs.

Appendix A	Student Reactions to Instruction and Courses
Appendix B	Evaluation by Students
Appendix C	Mid-Semester Evaluation of Instructors
Appendix D	Small Group Instructional Diagnosis
Appendix E	Student Appraisal of Advising
Appendix F	Classroom Observation Feedback
Appendix G	Classroom Observation Report
Appendix H	Review of Teaching Materials
Appendix I	Self-Reflection
Appendix J	Portfolio Assessment Guide
Appendix K	Appraisal of Research/Publication
Appendix L	Evaluating Faculty Service

Appendix A
Student Reactions to Instruction and Courses

SHORT FORM - STUDENT REACTIONS TO INSTRUCTION AND COURSES   (i) **IDEA** CENTER

Institution:	Instructor:
Course Number:	Time and Days Class Meets:

IMPORTANT!   USE NO.2 PENCIL ONLY

Proper Marks ●●●●●●

Improper Marks ⊙⊘⊗⊖◗⊕

Twelve possible learning objectives are listed below, not all of which will be relevant in this class. Describe the amount of progress you made on each (even those not pursued in this class) by using the following scale:

1-No apparent progress
2-Slight progress; I made small gains on this objective.
3-Moderate progress; I made some gains on this objective.
4-Substantial progress; I made large gains on this objective.
5-Exceptional progress; I made outstanding gains on this objective.

Progress on:

1. ① ② ③ ④ ⑤ Gaining factual knowledge (terminology, classifications, methods, trends)
2. ① ② ③ ④ ⑤ Learning fundamental principles, generalizations, or theories
3. ① ② ③ ④ ⑤ Learning to *apply* course material (to improve thinking, problem solving, and decisions)
4. ① ② ③ ④ ⑤ Developing specific skills, competencies, and points of view needed by professionals in the field most closely related to this course
5. ① ② ③ ④ ⑤ Acquiring skills in working with others as a member of a team
6. ① ② ③ ④ ⑤ Developing creative capacities (writing, inventing, designing, performing in art, music, drama, etc.)
7. ① ② ③ ④ ⑤ Gaining a broader understanding and appreciation of intellectual/cultural activity (music, science, literature, etc.)
8. ① ② ③ ④ ⑤ Developing skill in expressing myself orally or in writing
9. ① ② ③ ④ ⑤ Learning how to find and use resources for answering questions or solving problems
10. ① ② ③ ④ ⑤ Developing a clearer understanding of, and commitment to, personal values
11. ① ② ③ ④ ⑤ Learning to analyze and *critically* evaluate ideas, arguments, and points of view
12. ① ② ③ ④ ⑤ Acquiring an interest in learning more by asking my own questions and seeking answers

For the remaining questions, use the following code:

1=Definitely False	2=More False Than True	3=In Between	4=More True Than False	5=Definitely True

13. ① ② ③ ④ ⑤ As a rule, I put forth more effort than other students on academic work.
14. ① ② ③ ④ ⑤ My background prepared me well for this course's requirements.
15. ① ② ③ ④ ⑤ I really wanted to take this course regardless of who taught it.
16. ① ② ③ ④ ⑤ As a result of taking this course, I have more positive feelings toward this field of study.
17. ① ② ③ ④ ⑤ Overall, I rate this instructor an excellent teacher.
18. ① ② ③ ④ ⑤ Overall, I rate this course as excellent.

EXTRA QUESTIONS
If your instructor has extra questions, answer them in the space designated below (questions 19-38).

19. ① ② ③ ④ ⑤	24. ① ② ③ ④ ⑤	29. ① ② ③ ④ ⑤	34. ① ② ③ ④ ⑤
20. ① ② ③ ④ ⑤	25. ① ② ③ ④ ⑤	30. ① ② ③ ④ ⑤	35. ① ② ③ ④ ⑤
21. ① ② ③ ④ ⑤	26. ① ② ③ ④ ⑤	31. ① ② ③ ④ ⑤	36. ① ② ③ ④ ⑤
22. ① ② ③ ④ ⑤	27. ① ② ③ ④ ⑤	32. ① ② ③ ④ ⑤	37. ① ② ③ ④ ⑤
23. ① ② ③ ④ ⑤	28. ① ② ③ ④ ⑤	33. ① ② ③ ④ ⑤	38. ① ② ③ ④ ⑤

Appendix B
Evaluation by Students

Instructor _____

Course _____

Date _____

1) What have been the most positive aspects of the course?
   Are there any particular aspects you found beneficial?

2) What have been the negative features of this course?
   Are there any particular aspects you have disliked?

3) Were the instructor's handouts and review sheets useful?
   Should they be used in this course in the future?

4) Would you recommend using the same textbook(s)?

5) Should the same grading format (exams, assignments,
   discussion) be used?

6) Does the instructor create an environment in which you feel
   comfortable participating? Is the classroom environment
   friendly? Is it respectful of diverse opinions?

7) Do you find the instructor approachable and open to
   questions, both during class and in office hours?

8) Does the instructor come to class well prepared?

9) Is the material presented clearly and effectively?

10) Has your interest in the topics discussed increased due to the class materials and instruction? (If necessary, explain.)

11) Would you consider taking another class with this instructor or would you recommend this course or this instructor to another student? (If necessary, explain.)

12) What is your overall assessment of the instructor's teaching performance? (Be as specific as possible.)

Adapted from Sokolon, M. (2003).

Appendix C
Mid-Semester Evaluation of Instructors

Below are examples of evaluations that are useful for mid-semester feedback. Choose the one that best reflects your teaching goals and teaching styles.

Example 1

Please complete the following sentences:

1) The instructor is _____

   _____

2) The textbook is _____

   _____

3) The lectures are _____

   _____

4) The quizzes are _____

   _____

5) The assignments are _____

   _____

Adapted from Lucas S. G. (2001). Departmental orientation programs for teaching assistants. In L. R. Prieto & S. A. Meyers (Eds.), *The teaching assistant training handbook: How to prepare TAs for the responsibilities* (pp. 25–50). Stillwater, OK: New Forums Press.

Example 2

Please respond to the following items and add any additional comments.

1) The reason(s) I took this course _____
   _____
   _____

2) The reason(s) other people took the course _____
   _____
   _____

3) The people who are doing well in the course are those _____
   _____
   _____

4) The people who are not doing well in the course are those ____
   _____
   _____

5) Changes that would make the course better for me are _____
   _____
   _____

6) Other comments, complaints, or ideas _____
   _____
   _____

Example 3

Please complete the following questions and add any additional comments or complaints.

1) The thing I like *most* about this course is _____

_____

_____

2) The thing I like *least* about this course is _____

_____

_____

3) If I could change anything about this course, I would change __

_____

_____

4) If only there would be _____

_____

_____

5) If only the textbook was _____

_____

_____

6) The instructor should _____

_____

_____

7) One thing I like about the instructor is _____

_____

_____

8) Concerning my being prepared to take the midterm exam I felt

_____

_____

9) I'd like to see more _____

_____

_____

Example 4

The following questions are particularly useful for collaborative classrooms.

1) What are *we* doing that is helping your learning?

2) What are *we* doing that is hindering your learning?

3) What can *we* do differently to improve your learning?

Examples 2, 3, and 4 developed by Seldin, P. (2002).

Example 5

Please complete the following information:

Course Name _____

Course Prefix and Number _____

Section Number _____

TA/Instructor _____

Please respond to the following questions by circling the number that best represents your response.

(1)	(2)	(3)	(4)	(5)	(6)
Strongly Disagree	Disagree	Neutral	Agree	Strongly Agree	Not Applicable

1) Prepares well for class   1 2 3 4 5 6

2) Makes oral presentations clearly   1 2 3 4 5 6

3) Presents material in an organized fashion   1 2 3 4 5 6

4) Encourages questions   1 2 3 4 5 6

5) Responds well to questions   1 2 3 4 5 6

6) Provides helpful feedback on course assignments   1 2 3 4 5 6

7) Shows concern that you are learning the material   1 2 3 4 5 6

8) Makes him/herself available outside of class   1 2 3 4 5 6

9) Demonstrates knowledge of the subject matter   1 2 3 4 5 6

10) Presents new material in an understandable way   1 2 3 4 5 6

11) Shows a willingness to help students who have difficulties   1 2 3 4 5 6

12) Communicates concepts, content, and issues clearly   1 2 3 4 5 6

(1)	(2)	(3)	(4)	(5)	(6)
Strongly Disagree	Disagree	Neutral	Agree	Strongly Agree	Not Applicable

13) Is approachable about course-related   1 2 3 4 5 6
    questions

14) Shows enthusiasm for the subject and   1 2 3 4 5 6
    for teaching

15) [Optional question for your particular   1 2 3 4 5 6
    course.]

Open-Ended Questions

1) What strengths has the instructor demonstrated that helped you to learn the course material? _____

_____

_____

2) What specific ways could the instructor improve how he or she teaches this course? _____

_____

_____

3) What other comments would you like to make regarding the instructor or the course? _____

_____

_____

Adapted from Lambert, L. M., Tice, S. L., & Featherstone, P. H. (Eds.). (1996). *University teaching: A guide for graduate students.* Syracuse, NY: Syracuse University Press.

Appendix D
Small Group Instructional Diagnosis

Small group instructional diagnosis is designed to assess components of the course the entire class feels are important. Discussions, led by trained facilitators, are conducted with students during class and feedback is provided to the instructor. Facilitators use the following questions to prompt student discussion:

1) For the first 10 minutes, you will write individually on the following topics:

   • What do you like most about the course/instructor?

   • What do you like least about the course/instructor and how could the instructor improve the course?

   • What could you do to make the course better for you and the instructor?

   For each of these please try to focus on specific behaviors, and describe why you like/dislike something, or why you think your suggested improvement would be beneficial.

2) For the next 20 minutes, you will have small group discussions of these topics.

   For each of the three topics listed above, I would like you to briefly describe your points. Only after all members of the group have spoken should you discuss the points raised. You should come up with two to three main points for each topic, with the group reaching consensus on the points.

3) For the final 30 minutes, we will have a large group discussion of these topics.

We will come to consensus on the most important points for the topics. I will then ask you to rate the extent to which you agree or disagree with each point. I will collect your individual and group responses but will not show them to your instructor. I will write a report that will go to your instructor.

Adapted from Creed, T. (1997, May). A model for consulting with faculty. *National Teaching and Learning Forum, 6*(4), 1–8.

Appendix E
Student Appraisal of Advising

Name of Advisor _____

Department _____

Date _____

Please circle the appropriate number.

How many times have you met (10 minutes or more) with your academic advisor this year?

    0 = I have not met with my advisor

    1 = One

    2 = Two or three

    3 = Four or five

    4 = Six or more

Rate your faculty advisor by circling the number that best expresses your view.

My advisor:	Low			High		n/a
1) Is friendly and responsive	1	2	3	4	5	n/a
2) Is readily available for academic advising	1	2	3	4	5	n/a
3) Has excellent communication skills	1	2	3	4	5	n/a
4) Is knowledgeable of course requirements and curriculum	1	2	3	4	5	n/a

	Low			High		n/a
5) Is helpful in solving academic problems	1	2	3	4	5	n/a
6) Strives to plan my academic program consistent with my interests and career objectives	1	2	3	4	5	n/a
7) Expresses interest in nonacademic problems	1	2	3	4	5	n/a
8) Has comprehensive knowledge of courses and requirements	1	2	3	4	5	n/a
9) Is responsive to student phone calls and email queries	1	2	3	4	5	n/a
10) Overall rating of faculty advisor	1	2	3	4	5	n/a

11) How has your faculty advisor been particularly helpful?

_____

_____

12) How could your faculty advisor be more helpful?

_____

_____

_____

Instrument developed by Seldin, C. A. (2005).

Appendix F
Classroom Observation Feedback

Instructor _____

Observer _____

Course _____ Lesson # _____ Topic _____

Date _____ Class Period _____ Room _____

Pre-Class Discussion	
Goals for class	
Plan to achieve goals	
Teaching/learning activities	
Student preparation/work due?	
Will this be typical class?	
Requested area of observation?	

Immediate Post-Class Discussion (Instructor's analysis of class)	
What went well?	
What did not go well?	
Change for next time?	
Observer Final Comments	

Observer Feedback	**Comments**
Knowledge	
Of topic	
Of students	
Organization	
Before class	
Introduction	
Topic progression	
Summary	

Observer Feedback	Comments
Use of time	
Skills and Techniques	
Enforces class rules	
Use of room	
Uses active learning	
Method of teaching	
Checks for understanding	
Visual/class aids	
Handles questions	
Communication	
Listens to students	
Rapport with students	
Heard/understood	
Gestures/movements	
Eye contact	
Student Performance	
Preparation	
Interaction	

Instrument developed by Hertel, J. P. (2003).

Appendix G
Classroom Observation Report

Instructor Evaluated _____ Course _____

Number of Students Present _____ Date _____

Evaluator(s) _____

Purpose
The purpose of this classroom observation is to provide a database for more accurate and equitable decisions on tenure, promotion, and merit increase and to improve faculty performance.

Instructions
Please consider each item carefully and assign the highest scores only for unusually effective performance.

Questions 12 and 13 have been deliberately left blank. You and the instructor being evaluated are encouraged to add your own items.

Each instructor should be observed on two occasions, and the observer(s) should remain in the classroom for the full class period.

It is suggested that the observer(s) arrange a pre-visit and post-visit meeting with the instructor.

Highest 5	4	Satisfactory 3	2	Lowest 1	Not Applicable n/a

	1) Defines objectives for the class presentation.
	2) Effectively organizes learning situations to meet the objectives of the class presentation.
	3) Uses instructional methods encouraging relevant student participation in the learning process.
	4) Uses class time effectively.
	5) Demonstrates enthusiasm for the subject matter.
	6) Communicates clearly and effectively to the level of the students.
	7) Explains important ideas simply and clearly.
	8) Demonstrates command of subject matter.
	9) Responds appropriately to student questions and comments.
	10) Encourages critical thinking and analysis.
	11) Consider the previous questions. How would you rate this instructor in comparison to others?
	12)
	13)
	14) Overall rating on the basis of classroom observation.

15) Would you recommend this instructor to students you are advising? (Please explain.)

_____

_____

16) What specific suggestions would you make concerning how this particular class could have been improved?

_____

_____

Did you have a pre-visit conference? _____

Post-visit conference? _____

Instrument developed by Seldin, P. (2004).

Appendix H
Review of Teaching Materials

Instructor Evaluated _____ Course _____

Evaluator(s) _____ Date _____

Purpose

The purpose of this review of teaching materials is to provide a database for more accurate and equitable decisions on tenure, promotion, and merit increase and to improve faculty performance.

Instructions

Please consider each item carefully and assign the highest scores only for unusually effective performance.

Highest		Satisfactory		Lowest	Not Applicable
5	4	3	2	1	n/a

	1) The course syllabus is current and relevant to the course outline.
	2) The syllabus is at an appropriate difficulty level.
	3) Homework assignments are effectively coordinated with the syllabus.
	4) The course objectives represent an appropriate mastery of the subject.
	5) The objectives dovetail with the department's overall objectives.

					Not
Highest		Satisfactory		Lowest	Applicable
5	4	3	2	1	n/a

	6) Examinations are consistent with the course objectives.
	7) Examinations reflect the important aspects of the subject.
	8) Teaching techniques are suitable to the course objectives.
	9) Textbooks and readings are appropriate to the course level.
	10) Technology is used appropriately.
	11) Course content is consistent with current knowledge of the subject.
	12) Course content offers a full and accurate representation of conflicting views and evidence.
	13) Overall rating of teaching materials.

Instrument developed by Miller, J. E., & Seldin, P. (2005).

Appendix I
Self-Reflection

Self-reflection, done in a systematic way, can lead to valuable insights and observations about one's teaching. Reflections may be captured through a teaching journal, a midcourse self-review, or a summative review. Writing about one's teaching experiences provides an opportunity to raise issues for reflection regarding both positive and negative aspects of a class. It can serve as the basis for improvement, refocusing of goals, and/or the development of a teaching portfolio. Self-reflection helps one make connections between theory and practice by exploring contradictions and compatibilities between what one wants to happen in class and what actually does happen.

Questions that may be useful in self-reflection include:

1) Was I really interested in the material I was teaching?
2) Was I enthusiastic in how I was teaching?
3) Was I well organized in my presentation of material?
4) Was my presentation well paced? Did I pause when I asked students to respond?
5) Could I have varied my presentation to make it more interesting?
6) Did the lesson/class proceed as I expected? If not, how did it change from my expectations? Was this a positive or negative result?
7) What strategies were helpful when students became confused?
8) What were the best aspects of the class?
9) What problems need to be addressed?
10) If I were to teach the course again, what would I do differently?

Instrument developed by Miller, J. E. (2005).

Appendix J
Portfolio Assessment Guide

SA	A	N	D	SD	NA
Strongly				Strongly	Not
Agree	Agree	Neutral	Disagree	Disagree	Applicable

1) The portfolio includes current information.	SA	A	N	D	SD	NA
2) There is coherence among the various components of the portfolio, revealing demonstrated effectiveness in practice tied to an articulated philosophy.	SA	A	N	D	SD	NA
3) The portfolio demonstrates performance consistent with departmental and institutional strategic priorities and missions.	SA	A	N	D	SD	NA
4) Valid documentation and evidence is provided.	SA	A	N	D	SD	NA
5) Multiple sources of information are included.	SA	A	N	D	SD	NA
6) Diverse and objective assessments are included.	SA	A	N	D	SD	NA
7) Empirical evidence that supports the narrative is included in the appendix.	SA	A	N	D	SD	NA

SA	A	N	D	SD	NA
Strongly Agree	Agree	Neutral	Disagree	Strongly Disagree	Not Applicable

8) The portfolio clearly and specifically reveals the relevance of professional development, research, and scholarship to performance	SA	A	N	D	SD	NA
9) The portfolio includes a core of agreed-upon seminal statements with accompanying evidence.	SA	A	N	D	SD	NA
10) The portfolio provides evidence of efforts to improve performance. There is evidence of improvement in methods, materials, evaluations, and goals.	SA	A	N	D	SD	NA
11) The portfolio includes materials and corroborative information about the professor's complex and varied roles.	SA	A	N	D	SD	NA
12) The portfolio makes a strong case, both in the narrative and in the documentation in the appendix, for the creativity and individuality of the professor's professional activities.	SA	A	N	D	SD	NA
13) The portfolio meets established length requirements.	SA	A	N	D	SD	NA

Specialty Items

The portfolio is best used for a specific purpose—to highlight teaching, to evaluate performance, to review administrative duties, or to present a more global perspective of one's professional accomplishments. To that end, additional questions may be included for use with specific types of portfolios.

For the teaching portfolio:

1) The teaching portfolio balances information from self, from others, and from products of student learning.
2) Diverse and objective assessments of teaching are included.
3) The portfolio makes a strong case for the use of specific teaching efforts with specific coursework and/or students.

For the professional portfolio:

1) The professional portfolio includes a balanced documentation of teaching, research/scholarship, and service.
2) The professional portfolio integrates information from self and others.
3) The professional portfolio presents a holistic examination of performance.

For the administrative portfolio:

1) The administrative portfolio integrates material from the administrator and others.
2) The administrative portfolio presents a holistic examination of performance.
3) The administrative portfolio includes performance evaluation data from multiple sources, not just the administrator's immediate supervisor.
4) The administrative portfolio is firmly rooted in the purposes and academic culture of this particular college or university.

Adapted by Miller, J. E. (2005) from Seldin, P. (2004). *The teaching portfolio: A practical guide to improved performance and promotion/tenure decisions* (3rd ed.). Bolton, MA: Anker.

Appendix K
Appraisal of Research/Publication

Faculty Member _____

Department _____ Date _____

Appraiser _____ Title _____

Please indicate your appraisal of the faculty member named above in regard to the following factors. Circle the number that most closely expresses your view.

	Low			High		Don't Know
1) How do you rate the adequacy of the research design (if applicable)?	1	2	3	4	5	X
2) How do colleagues outside the department rate the importance of the research study/publication?	1	2	3	4	5	X
3) Is the research study/publication closely related to the faculty member's area of teaching responsibility?	1	2	3	4	5	X
4) How do you rate the quality of this publication?	1	2	3	4	5	X
5) Was appropriate professional time and effort spent on this research study/publication?	1	2	3	4	5	X
6) Compared to others in the department, how do you rate the research/publication performance of this faculty member?	1	2	3	4	5	X

7) What is this faculty member's greatest strength with regard to research/publication? (Please elaborate.)

_____

_____

_____

_____

_____

8) What are his or her most serious shortcomings? (Please elaborate.)

_____

_____

_____

_____

_____

9) Additional comments. (Use reverse side if necessary.)

_____

_____

_____

_____

_____

Instrument developed by Seldin, P. (2005).

Appendix L
Evaluating Faculty Service

Faculty Member _____

Department _____ Date _____

Evaluator(s) _____ Title _____

The following elements reflect basic components of faculty service.

Please rate the faculty member named above by circling the number that most closely expresses your view.

	Low				High	Don't Know
1) Accepts service assignments willingly.	1	2	3	4	5	X
2) Completes an appropriate share of institutional service assignments.	1	2	3	4	5	X
3) Attends committee and faculty meeting regularly.	1	2	3	4	5	X
4) Maintains a professional and cooperative attitude in dealing with colleagues.	1	2	3	4	5	X
5) Serves effectively as a committee chairperson.	1	2	3	4	5	X
6) Is prompt in responding to colleagues' service-related emails and phone calls.	1	2	3	4	5	X
7) Actively supports departmental and institutional goals.	1	2	3	4	5	X

	Low			High		Don't Know
8) Positively contributes to assigned committees.	1	2	3	4	5	X
9) Is genuinely interested in assisting colleagues.	1	2	3	4	5	X
10) Willingly accepts leadership roles.	1	2	3	4	5	X
11) Overall rating of faculty service.	1	2	3	4	5	X

12) Nature of faculty assignments and services.

_____

_____

_____

_____

13) Additional comments.

_____

_____

_____

_____

Instrument developed by Seldin, P. (2005).

Index